CW00386431

But God ...!

Extraordinary intervention in an ordinary woman's life

by Doreen Moore

Barratt Ministries Publications

Acknowledgements

I would like to thank Bob and Ann Searle from I.G.O. for encouraging me to put pen to paper, and the Barratt Ministries team - Maurice Barratt for sharing the resources God has given him, Joanna Barratt for patiently typing my 'scrawl', and Alex Robertson for editing the text, designing the layout of the book and looking after all the publication process.

But God ...!
by Doreen Moore

British Library Cataloguing-in-Publication Data
A catalogue record for this book is available from the British Library

ISBN: 1 904592 07 4

Published 2004 by Barratt Ministries Puclications
114 Daisy Bank Road
Manchester M14 5QH, UK

Printed by Wright's of Sandbach
9 Old Middlewich Road
Sandbach, Cheshire CW11 1DP, UK

Chapter 1

Given to the Lord

"Doreen, I have given you to the Lord." These words were ingrained in my mind from early childhood. At first not understood ... just a nice story ... then the sense of frustration, before the unfolding of truth began to rise in my spirit. However, let's go back to the beginning. I rely on memory - details my mother told me again and again.

A traumatic start

At my parents' home in North Belfast I made my entry into this world, after a very traumatic birth which left my mother with torn nerves and unable to have any further children. I was a very sick baby, bringing up each feed shortly after receiving it, and soon lost weight. Specialist advice was sought and it was established that there was no entrance to my stomach. The doctor, a Christian, suggested he would operate and attempt to make a way for the food to reach the stomach. He could only give one chance in a hundred, as this had not been done before. He said that if I survived the surgery, one vomit would be fatal. My parents were devastated, but signed for the operation as the alternative was slow starvation to death. My mother related how she went home, fell on her bed sobbing, heartbroken, but into her mind came the remembrance of a Bible story from her Sunday School days, regarding Hannah, who longed for a child and cried to the Lord, saying, "If You give me a child I will give him back to You." My mother cried out to the Lord to spare my life, and she would give me back to Him. She heard an audible voice which said, "Don't fear, the child will live." A peace came with the assurance that her baby would not die. I was told the surgeon got on his knees before going into the theatre, asking God to guide his hand and give him wisdom. I came through the operation, but shortly after began to vomit. Mother said there was panic stations, but she stood by, thinking, "They don't know what I know - she will be all right!"

"Mind over matter"?

Mother shared this experience to her Minister, and was told, "It's just mind over matter - a trick of the mind because you were so distraught." Some months later when a doctor came from the hospital wanting to have information to help them to understand how a three-month-old baby was strong enough to survive the ordeal, my mother did not give testimony of her prayer, nor give God the glory. Nor did she walk in the revelation that God could do miracles, nor look for His intervention for her own health problems. Scripture is correct when it says, "death and life are in the power of the tongue."

Throughout my life I had very loving parents and a very secure childhood. Looking back, I realise my mother was over-protective. I was not allowed to go to the public swimming baths or have books from the library, for fear of germs. In spite of this I managed to catch every disease available, and this continued into my teens.

My parents were members of a local Presbyterian Church and attended on a regular basis, taking me with them. In the light of the promise they had made, they did their best to bring me up with a reverence and fear of God according to the light they had at that time. I was told Bible stories, was disciplined for disobedience, never harshly, but enough for me to learn the lesson and to have values instilled into me that have stayed with me all these years. On Sundays and 'holy' days I was not allowed to play with toys or run about playing games. "It's the Lord's Day, and if you aren't a good girl God won't love you!"

I cannot emphasise enough how happy my childhood was, and the desire was born in me to please God. As a young teenager I had a mental list of things I would not do, or places I would not go. I remember one occasion when I was allowed out with an older girl, the daughter of friends of my parents, I stood for a considerable time outside a pub rather than go inside, as I didn't want to displease God.

No resentment

I have never resented my upbringing. Rather I have been grateful to the grace of God that I didn't get caught up in sin and the worldliness of my day. I am thankful for a loving mother who remembered her vow to God and did all she knew how to keep her promise. The one way she felt this could be fulfilled was by me marrying a Presbyterian Minister, and when I came of age to be boy-conscious this was frustrating. My constant cry was, "If a Minister was the last man on earth, I would not marry him!"

My parents made sacrifices so that I could have a good education at a college which was situated in a different part of the city from my home. This meant I had friends who were not near neighbours. This was an important fact, I believe it was part of God's plan for my life and set the scene for a future event. I wanted to be a primary school teacher, but because I was not able to distinguish notes on the piano, and I was advised music was a necessary qualification, I abandoned that dream and left school. With only my junior certificate I went on to train as an acomptometer operator, and was soon working for my living.

Chapter 2

Decision Time

I still visited my school friends, and on alternate Saturdays we visited each other's homes, had tea, and then went out for the evening. On one such occasion, when I arrived at my friend's, her father said there was a mission in their church, and Valerie (his daughter) was to attend at least once. This was the final night and she was to go. I could go with her or I could return home. I decided I did not want to go home, so there I was in church on a Saturday night. The speaker was from the People's Church in Toronto, Canada. I cannot recall what his message was but I will never forget one verse of scripture which stated, "all our righteousness is like filthy rags." I can still bring to mind the awfulness of that truth breaking into my thinking, and all the realisation that every effort and endeavour to be good and to please God was just seen as a bunch of dirty old rags. My heart responded and I left my friends to make my way down to the altar. With tears streaming down my cheeks, I confessed my sin and accepted CHRIST into my life. I still have the card I signed that night making a covenant with God to follow Him and to serve His Church to advance His Kingdom. It is dated

28th September, 1949. I had celebrated my sixteenth birthday just a few days previously.

I went home and told my mother what had happened. Looking back I am not sure that she understood, but anything that would bring her promise about was all right with her! Then I experienced my first setback. I related the incident to a Minister and was told there was no need to go "over the top". I was fine as I was and did not need to go to extremes. This resulted in me carrying on as before, and with no further teaching I had no spiritual growth. *But God ..!* - He had His hand on me.

Around this time my grandmother came to live with us. I was very close to her. Not many weeks after she moved in she died very suddenly and I grieved her passing - so much so that my mother made plans for me to go out more, and arranged that the son of a friend of hers would take me to the choir practice. Because he was good-looking and quite a bit older than me, I had no objections! So I joined the church choir, and mindful of my lack of singing ability I mimed the words. The choir had entered into a hymn-singing competition and needed more bass singers, so the Minister on his visitations in the parish was always ready to recruit anyone to the choir, and because of his endeavours a new young man joined.

Another milestone

On the night of the competition, we travelled by coach to another town some miles away and we were allowed to bring a friend. I remember how devastated I felt when my neighbourly escort turned up with a young woman who was his girlfriend. He had given me no reason for any expectations, it was only my own romantic mind, but I did feel annoyed. When the new boy came to talk to me and ask if he could see me home I was only too pleased to say yes, even if only to show my escort he was not needed. This proved to be another important milestone in my life.

So life took a different turn. I began dating Billy and getting to know him. My father wasn't all that pleased, as Billy worked as an electrician in the aircraft factory. Some month previous I had worked in the wages office of the same firm and Dad asked me to get another job. He didn't want me to meet anyone 'beneath my station'. As an obedient daughter I applied and got a job as junior costing clerk in a linen firm. But now it was different. I was falling in love and was not so willing to comply to his wishes.

Inferiority complex

So we went out together, picture houses, walking, talking, and I discovered that Billy wasn't the happiest of people. He was very unsure of himself. In fact, he had quite an inferiority complex. His mother never had a good word to say about him and never expected anyone else to think well of him either. This was not just Billy's explanation, for in later weeks I was in her company and realised that what he said was true. He told me he felt like taking his own life, but things were different now because of me. Even though I had no teaching on the subject I had an uneasiness deep down as to whether it was right to go out with him as I was a Christian and he wasn't. However, such thoughts were stifled and the relationship began to grow. He did not see any way for an engagement as he handed his pay packet to his mother and only received pocket money in return, and my father insisted that at eighteen I was far too young for any serious relationship.

Several weeks passed, then something important happened. A workmate led Billy to the Lord during his lunch break. This should have been a real time of rejoicing, but it had the opposite effect and friction crept in. Billy was not only led to the Lord, but he was counselled to live separated from the world, so now Bible Studies and Prayer Meetings were on the agenda. Because of Billy I was willing to go too, but suddenly my mother was not happy. It was spoiling my fun. In her eyes there hadn't been anything wrong with our social life! But Billy was adamant. He wanted the Prayer Meetings, and as I wanted to be with him, meetings it was! On Saturday nights we started to attend the Youth for Christ meetings in Belfast's YMCA Hall and there we met John Wesley White from Canada. This turned out to be another of God's appointments, but the significance wasn't apparent until some years later.

Accepted at last

A couple of years passed and things began to change - at least on the surface. I was accepted by Billy's mother and she said we could get married. In fact, she had a house which was rented out and we could ask the people to vacate, providing the owner needed it as his residence. She indicated she was happy for Billy to have it. Actually, unbeknown to him, he was part-owner according to the way things were left at his father's death. My father gave his permission that I could be engaged on my twentieth birthday. He had come to the conclusion we were serious about each other and had decided that, even though Billy was not the suitor he had hoped for, he was a man of integrity.

Some weeks before my birthday, something went wrong with my left knee and I had so much pain that I could not walk. I became a patient in Musgrave Park Hospital and underwent a series of painful cortisone injections inserted under the knee cap. This treatment was not successful and the orthopaedic specialist told my father he would operate to remove the knee cap and stretch the muscle to cover the knee joint. The side-effect of this drug meant that I had put on weight - practically a stone overnight! In spite of this Billy and I visited the jewellers to choose an engagement ring on my birthday. With the confidence of youth we began to plan our wedding and decided it would be the following year. A relative of Billy's had died and left him some money, so it was all systems go! Within weeks we had a date set, and the church and reception booked. In all these arrangements there was one big flaw ... we neglected to consult God. I honestly don't think either of us knew that we should, but I now believe that God did have plans for us and He needed to intervene.

Divine intervention

Divine intervention there was. Billy lost his job. Many were laid off because a plane had crashed on its trial flight. We put our savings into a little shop. This coincided with the legal proceedings concluding and the house becoming vacant. Billy's mother changed her tack. She decided she would live in the house herself, unless Billy was willing to buy her share. This took all our savings and crippled us for putting stock in the shop. I am not sure what lay behind her decision, but I recall that I went to visit her and tried to find out. That was a mistake. It ended in a row and Billy's bags were packed. She said I had made him religious and she wanted nothing more to do with him. In fact, he was not her son anymore.

These events resulted in the cancellation of all our wedding plans. My mother found Billy some digs with a neighbour in our street, but as Billy could not afford to pay his landlady, my mother gave him his meals. Right at this time James White came to Belfast from America to hold salvation and healing services, and Billy decided to attend one afternoon whilst I was at work. What he saw and heard was mind-blowing. So he asked me to go with him that night.

A hostile reaction

I did not like the meeting. It was noisy, people saying things out loud, and I felt uncomfortable with his preaching - Christ first! I was afraid of the things I saw but did not understand. I was Presbyterian and was not going back. But the next night saw us there again, witnessing miracles. With my own eyes I saw people get up out of wheelchairs. Turned eyes of children, when prayed for in the name of Jesus, straightened in an instant. Billy decided this was the answer to my mother's need. She had been a semi-invalid since my birth and had spent some time in a nervous diseases hospital. So he acquired a prayer card for her and stood in the queue on her behalf whilst she waited in a nearby cafe until the doors opened. These meetings were drawing crowds of people and they came hours before the service started.

My mother's reaction was the same as mine - she did not like it, and decided that James White was paying people to fall down when he touched them, or perhaps he was a hypnotist! Nevertheless she went back, Billy telling her of the many miracles, and he believed she could be healed. My father would not have anything to do with this. He was upset that we went, we should not go anywhere but to our own church. This obstinacy was to stay for many years, *but God* ... That will come later!

The crowd grew too large for the Ulster Hall in the middle of Belfast and the venue moved to the Kings Hall on the outskirts of the city. I learned at a later date that James White had been given a vision of himself in this hall and was told to go. He obeyed the voice of the Lord and, although he had major setbacks and opposition from the churches, he persevered until he saw the fulfilment. I remember the police being there to direct the traffic. Cars and coaches came from all over the province, the services were relayed to nearby halls, and yet still more came. Billy, my mum and I were there one evening. By this time my mother had remembered that God had spoken to her and saved my life, and she decided that God was able, in spite of what she thought of the preacher. But she would not fall on the floor, that wasn't necessary (and besides, she had on her good coat!)

"Wait for the power of God"

When the prayer line was called there were too many people, so James White said he did not need to lay hands on them, it was not his power. They should believe that when he called on the name of Jesus, Jesus would heal. My mother believed and went forward. She was halfway down the hall, nowhere near the platform, people pressing up against her, and James White prayed "Wait for the power of God ... wait ... here it comes ... In the name of JESUS". It was awesome. A power just swept across the whole place, people were slain and fell on the floor, no-one about to catch them, almost but not quite falling on top of one another ... and my mum spread out on the floor in her good coat! The meeting was dismissed, people began to leave and still my mum was on the floor. Billy decided we needed to get her up as we were in danger of missing the last bus home. So we did, but she was intoxicated with the presence of God. We had to support her, one on either side, get to the bus stop and on to the bus, set her down on a seat, overhearing other passengers being sorry for the young couple having such a drunk mother. Talk about being embarrassed ... Especially as we were not sure what was going on either! My mother was healed on the 19th October, 1954 and did not need to continue with the medication she was supposed to have for the rest of her life. And she stayed healed for the rest of her days.

Encouragement and healing

This testimony was a great encouragement to me. Billy and I returned to Kings Hall on Sunday afternoon (24th), and on that occasion the Evangelist said there was an anointing for healing of all knee complaints, so I responded, and without hands being laid on me I also experienced the mighty power of God, and ended up flat on my back with a burning sensation in my knee. I was healed and did not need the operation. The affliction never touched any other part of my body, and nearly 50 years later I have no knee problems.

I can't quite remember if it was the same afternoon, or a different day, but I remember distinctly that the preacher made a call for young men to surrender their lives to God and follow a call to be in full-time ministry. Billy responded, he would go into the ministry. I was reminded of my careless words - "if a minister was the last man on earth I would not marry him!"

Then it was over, it was time for James White to return home, he had accomplished his God-given commission and had seen many many people saved, healed and delivered. Many were called into the ministry, and it was a near-revival, the impact of which has lasted until this day. I personally know men and women in service for God who were influenced in those meetings.

Chapter 3

Life In The Spirit

The meetings with James White left Billy and I with many questions and a deep hunger for something - we didn't even know what. We had heard many references to the Holy Spirit, we had heard strange tongues, what was baptism? Over the next weeks we spent our time together searching the Bible for answers, until a desperation set in. We needed to know! "Have you received the Holy Spirit since you believed?" (Acts 19:2) was also a challenge.

Then one afternoon Billy was in the city centre and he saw a man he recognised had been an usher in the crusade, so he stopped him and explained what had happened to us, and the hunger we had to learn more; and this wonderful stranger gave Billy his address and invited us both to visit him. I can still remember the excitement, the wonder, and we went to his home. This man and his wife made us so welcome, they spent a couple of hours opening up the scriptures to us, and offered to pray for us to receive the baptism of the Spirit. So we prayed - this was a new experience for me - and a fear set in. It was a completely new thing for me to praise the Lord out loud, and it seemed that my throat became paralysed. Then this brother prayed and 'bound' the spirit of fear, and a wonderful warmth flooded over me, my tongue was free to utter praise which soon became a new utterance.

At this point our hostess pointed out the fact that if we didn't leave now we would miss our connecting bus home. They lived on the opposite side of the city, and we needed two buses. Billy and I were in agreement, we wouldn't leave until we had both received, even if it meant walking, and facing my father's wrath for not being home at the appointed time. So back to prayer, and moments later, Billy was also speaking with a new tongue. We grabbed our coats and ran!

God was so good, the bus we needed in city centre was late leaving and we were able to board it. We were elated, we were walking on air, we were rejoicing, we hopped, skipped all down the avenue when we got off the bus. Billy said afterwards that when I had received the Spirit he felt jealous, and said to the Lord, "If Doreen can receive, then I'm not going until I do". I left Billy and entered my home feeling ready to burst, to have my father say, "You're late, wash the supper dishes before you go to bed."

"It's not Presbyterian!"

My uncles and aunts on my father's side had emigrated to Australia, my paternal grandparents were dead, but my mother had two brothers and a sister, and with their spouses we were a very close family, visiting each other's homes, sharing birthdays, etc., any excuse for a party. I have two cousins both younger than me. My uncles were elders in their churches, and all the family sided with my dad: we were being led into something which wasn't right, it wasn't Presbyterian!! My mother quietly backed us. "Hugh", she said to my dad, "I've given Doreen to the Lord." My dad's one desire in life was to keep mum happy, so he would back off.

Then Billy made a monumentous decision. He had already stopped smoking, but now he decided he would not sell any more cigarettes in his shop. Well, what a thing to say, after all it was a sweet and tobacconist, with light groceries. It was the cigarettes which brought people into the shop, and it wasn't doing well as it was. My family all gave their advice ... "You're committing trade suicide. What's wrong with smoking anyway? WE smoke!" But Billy was adamant. He would do what he felt was right. As for me, anything Billy did was right! My mum's contribution: "Let God work it out!" Billy had a staunch ally in my mum, they became very close and spent time talking together, sharing the things Billy was experiencing in his new walk with God.

Believers' baptism

Around the same time Billy made a second decision. He would be baptized in water. My mum and I agreed, we wanted to do so as well. One problem, we belonged to a church who didn't baptize adults, only sprinkled babies. Never mind, God would make a way. Then Billy saw an advert in the newspaper: a church across town was having a baptismal service, and they included a telephone number in the ad. So Billy phoned and boldly explained that we were Presbyterians, didn't want to be anything else, but he could see from the Bible that Jesus was baptised in water, and he, his fiancée and her mother also wanted this experience. This unknown minister was so gracious. After establishing that we did know Jesus Christ as Saviour, he was happy to help without us having to make any commitment to his church. On the 22nd January, 1956, Billy was immersed, and as he came up out of the water he began to dance. The people erupted in praise. "The hand of the Lord is on this young man," was the minister's response. Three weeks later we returned, and mum and I were also baptized. My dad would not attend, sadly he did not approve.

Chapter 4

Commissioned

Since we had been baptised in the Holy Spirit, it had been our desire to witness, so we visited friends, talked of our experiences, and prayed with them for healing. Our enthusiasm was great. We saw many healed. One lady with a cancerous growth on the bridge of her nose was prayed for, and the growth withered and fell off. The skin underneath was like new.

One evening we set out to visit another friend, and as we walked we began to discuss the call on Billy's life. He told me he didn't know what to do. He did not know how to proceed, he did not know the Bible. I remember clearly how I replied. "Billy, God caused you to meet a man when we wanted the Holy Spirit, He found a church for baptism in water, I think He will have you meet someone else who can help." The words had just left my mouth when a hand came on Billy's shoulder, and as we turned, there was John Wesley White, whom we had met a few years before. What we hadn't realised was the fact that we had been so engrossed in our conversation we had not turned into the street we intended to, but had carried on and were now in the city centre - face to face with another of God's messengers. John asked how things were and the reply was given: "Naturally speaking, they couldn't be worse. I've lost my job, been put out of my mother's home, disinherited, cancelled our wedding plans, put savings into a shop that's not doing well, in fact I owe money. But spiritually, it couldn't be better. God has called me into ministry, I don't know what you think of this but I've been filled with the Holy Spirit, speak in tongues, baptized in water John's immediate reply was, "I know where you should be - the Full Gospel Bible Institute, Eston, Canada. I will give you the address of the Principal and I will write to him on your behalf with a recommendation. It's good to see you. God bless you and open the doors you need." And off he went!

Bible College

So Billy applied for college. It was God, it did not matter that it was in Canada. He didn't have money. It did not matter that he would leave me. It was God's will - end of discussion!

But it was not the end of the discussion as far as my family were concerned. They had never heard of such a hare-brained idea. Billy had taken leave of his senses. I should consider what I was letting myself in for. Anyway, it wouldn't happen. "He's broke, how will he get there?" "He hasn't got the education." "You don't know enough about it, he could be brainwashed." And so it went on. My mum: "Let's just trust God!" She had been a tailoress before her marriage, so now she decided to do some dressmaking, and the money earned would go to help Billy.

The troubles deepened for us. The predictions regarding the shop were coming to pass. There was less trade and the money owed to the wholesale merchant was increasing. To make matters worse, the house we were supposed to live in had been broken into, and everything like power sockets and door handles were stolen. We could not get it fixed - no money. We could not live in it either. So Billy stayed with our neighbour, and she let him stay without paying rent.

Then, towards the end of February, 1956, a letter came from Canada. Billy had been accepted as a student and was to attend in October. I can't remember the amount of money he needed for the three-year course, nor the fare for the journey from Belfast to Eston in Saskatchewan. It was a lot! But Billy was going. God would supply. I had many different emotions. On the one hand I could see the hand of God in all of this. I don't think I was especially thinking of mum's promise to the Lord. I was very much involved, being in love with Billy, and as long as it was Billy and me I would be satisfied. Neither of us relished the thought of being parted with so many miles in between.

Thrown on the Lord

I was still working in my job in the linen firm, and received promotion and a good pay packet, but I gave my money to my mum and received pocket money from her. Nothing changed over the next two months. We did spend time in prayer, Billy especially, as he wasn't busy in the shop. On the 7th May, another decision: Billy would give up the shop, advertise the premises, give up the house, and throw himself completely on the Lord. The following evening we were due to go with my parents to visit friends, but we asked their permission to stay in my home to pray rather than accompany them. This was granted, and so we were on our knees in my living room crying out to God, taking it in turns to tell Him our woes, our hopes, and asking for His intervention. That evening is another event which I will always remember. There was such a presence in the room. I had never experienced anything like it before - it was so awesome that we could not continue speaking. I felt I should not even lift my head or look around. Then, after a period of silence, I found myself speaking in an unknown tongue, something I had not done since the night I received the Holy Spirit. Immediately I stopped, Billy began to speak in English, but in a cultured voice, saying words to the effect we need not fear, God was in control, he had called us and would supply the need, just lean on Him. Then the presence left.

We just sat trying to take it all in - perhaps even questioning the experience. Then my mum and dad came in, wanting to know who had been in the house. Apparently they had returned via the back door. Reaching the living room they had heard a voice they didn't recognise, but heard the message. This was a great blessing. We doubted no more, and were elated that God had visited us. My dad had nothing to say.

Answers to prayer

Within days, things happened. First, my uncle by marriage said he had a friend who would repair the house and wait until it was sold before he received payment. Someone responded to the ad for the shop, came to view, and decided he would have the premises. It hadn't any good will, so the existing stock had to be cleared before Billy vacated. I decided to help out, so I asked friends and neighbours if they would purchase some of the goods.

Next day I got a phone call from Billy: could I come out of work, he needed my help. The man had come back to discuss some details, and as an afterthought he asked what was happening to the stock. Billy replied he was hoping to sell it. The man said, "Make a list of the wholesale price and I will buy it." Thus I was needed to take stock and price it, etc. I also had to say sorry to the Lord for interfering and I had the embarrassing task of explaining to all my friends that there would be no goods to sell them.

Plea for reconciliation

Just one thing remained in Billy's mind - his mother. Perhaps she really wanted the house. He could not go to see her himself. My family did not think he needed to, he had paid her a fair price for her portion, but again Billy was determined. We had a new minister in our church, a believer who was sympathetic towards us. He said he would go and speak to Mrs. Moore - after all, she was a member of his flock, even though she had never attended the church. He also wanted to plead for reconciliation between mother and son.

It was not to be. But she did say she did not want the house. So Billy had a clear conscience about selling it. Unknown to us, it was already sold even while the minister was with Mrs. Moore. It had been on the market with instructions that it would not go until he had his mother's answer, so with that in mind, the agent put a higher price on it, saying that any prospective buyer would make an offer, and that would give the time needed. But it didn't quite work out according to plan. The buyer said, "I will buy at the asking price," and put the required deposit on the desk there and then. All was well, God was in control. He was supplying every need. So a very jubilant Billy had money to pay off his debts, purchase his ticket for ship and rail ... Eston, here he comes! I, too, was elated in seeing the hand of God, but how I would miss Billy. He was my life. So plans were made and the money was transferred to a bank in Canada. A "sterling block" was placed on him, meaning that he could not have any more money sent out nor could he earn any money should he return to the U.K. during the three years course in Eston. This was to have repercussions at a later date.

Answer to the heart cry

Billy was still unhappy regarding his mother. We prayed much for this situation. Some time before he was due to sail I was awakened in the early hours, and on answering the door found a policeman on the doorstep, looking for Mr. Moore. Knowing something was amiss, my dad went with the officer to Billy's lodging, and was there to hear the officer say that Billy's mother had died in hospital.

We were devastated - *but God...!!* It was only next day that Billy learned what had happened. His mother had taken ill, had called out the window to a passing neighbour and asked for her friend to be alerted. She threw the key when her friend came a few minutes later, and she told her friend she had a change of heart. She had treated Billy wrongly, she said, and asked if this lady would please tell him he was her son. Some days after the funeral, other people spoke to Billy and they had heard from Mrs. Moore that he was going to college, and that she was proud of him.

So, in the midst of the grief, the knowledge of a heart change. Others said she had been a new woman for days, cheerful, just different. Who can tell just what change there was. Only Eternity will reveal the answer to that. It was clear that God had indeed answered Billy's heart cry, and had undertaken in a wonderful way.

Chapter 5

Goodbye Billy...

When things started to come together for Billy's trip to Canada, a lot of voices in our family circle - very critical voices at first - were silenced. My mum organised a party for Billy, we would not see him for three years, then we would plan our wedding. She hired a hall, invited the family, neighbours, our Christian friends, to say goodbye, and to wish him well. It was a happy time, but the parting came nearer. Billy bought me a locket with his photograph, and had written, "With Love, Billy" in it. I still have it, though I have needed to replace the photo and go over the writing as it has faded with time.

Then came the day. October 11th, 1956, he walked up the gangplank in Belfast Docks, bound for Liverpool, and then to set sail to Montreal. Goodbye Billy. I was heartbroken, but God was on my case, not quite the way I would have expected.

It was not long before the Lord was challenging me. Was I willing to put Him first? What if He wanted me to do or go somewhere without Billy? I agonised over this. I had to look deep into my own heart. I had to face the fact that Billy was the most important person in my life. The

Lord faced me with the question, "Are you willing to follow Me - go where I send you, even without Billy?" I agonised over this! I wept! But had to make the decision - and I became willing to give Billy up, and put God in His rightful place in my life. I was willing to offer my 'Isaac' as a sacrifice to the Lord Jesus! With my decision came peace.

Then came a new thought. I can't remember the time sequence, but the thought was there! Why don't you go to Bible School? Followed by the scripture which has been 'my verse' throughout the years, "You did not choose Me, but I have chosen you and appointed you that you should go and bear fruit and that your fruit should remain" (John 15:16).

"Apply!"

Letters were going back and forth almost daily. Billy was lovesick, or homesick. I told him about the thought of Bible School, for this time I prayed and wanted the Lord's will on the matter. Billy made enquiries at Eston, prayer was there as well, then the word came, "apply". I felt it was right. It was a very different matter for my parents, now it was their one and only daughter contemplating a move to far-off fields, very different from living down the road. But their permission was given, on the condition I would be married first. I was accepted to begin the studies October 1957. Billy made plans to return home after the first year was finished. Just one problem - where would he live? What would he live on? Remember the sterling block!

Before he went to Canada he had a good influence on his cousin and his wife. They came into the Pentecostal truth, and in gratefulness opened their home to Billy, fed and looked after him. I had saved some of my pocket money, but nothing to cover what would be needed, then my mum and dad handed me a bank book they had saved systematically over the years from my pay packet towards my wedding, but now they said I could use it as I liked. We had a lovely wedding, but did keep costs down so I could also have the things necessary for cold Canadian winters.

There were expenses the groom was expected to look after, and Billy was determined to trust God. The first provision was when we went to get the licence. We had to go to another Presbyterian minister in the district and he needed to fill out forms, etc. The nature of Billy's employment was one such question, but it was an opportunity to witness to him, and the whole testimony was told. The man was interested and when all was completed, it came to payment time, and he said, "I want to be the first with a wedding present. You don't need to pay for your licence."

God's gift

My mum was making my wedding dress and those for the bridesmaids, my two cousins. I dearly wanted a nice going-away outfit, and had searched the shops for my desire, but when I couldn't find it, came home disappointed. Later that same evening a gentleman from the church came to the house with a parcel. "My wife wants to give you a gift, she had this in the house, hope it will be of use to you," and he was gone. When I opened the parcel it was material the exact colour I had wanted and the exact yardage needed to make the costume. 7th September, 1957, my mum and dad's Silver Wedding Anniversary, was our wedding day. We had about three weeks before leaving for Canada, and we decided the voyage would be our honeymoon. Our best man lent us his caravan for a few days, and we spent the rest of our time in my parents house. Then it was goodbye time. This was hard for me. My mum could trace God's hand in everything, she knew she had given me to the Lord, but dad, his pain because I was leaving, was hard for me to see, even though he had not agreed with all things, his love for me and mine for him never diminished.

Chapter 6

Canada

So started another chapter. I had very mixed emotions - sadness leaving my parents - joy at being Billy's wife. And excitement of the adventure, the luxury of "The Empress of England" Line voyage, new cities - Quebec, Montreal - aboard the train for two days and two nights, travelling through Ontario, Manitoba and half way across Saskatchewan. The landscape unlike anything I'd ever seen. The vastness - miles without apparent habitation. Stopping at little settlements - able to stretch our legs - sample food at the cafe - heard the accents when spoken to. At one such stop, I looked out of the window and was horrified to see the train move forward. I remember my reaction - "Billy, Billy, the train's going and all our belongings are on board!" And the embarrassment when told, "It's only going to take water on board!"

I wrote so many letters to my mum and dad, and asked them to keep them. Wisdom! - as I have been able to read them and refresh my memory. One thing stood out above all else, my reliance on God - what a change to my attitude. Billy and I purposed that our life would start with Bible reading and praying together, and this continued throughout our years together.

We reached Saskatoon, met by the church folk, and continued our journey to Eston. Billy had described what it was like, but I was not prepared for what I saw! Me - a city girl - and now only large wheat silos. A wooden building at a short platform was the train station. A post office, a drug store, a bank, a cafe, a couple of stores (small shops), two churches, a few streets. No tarmac, no trees, no hills - just flat, flat, flat. But what a welcome. Billy was well thought of, now here was Doreen. Not just a photograph, but for real.

Our first home

We were the first married students at the college which was situated on the edge of town. It had houses for the staff, two dormitories, a chapel which housed the classrooms, kitchen, dining hall, laundry, etc. - but no married quarters. So the Principal had rented a small house on the main street. It was used in the summer months by a grain merchant and when the wheat was harvested he left Eston. This was so different from home - a one-storey wooden building, with large living room and a heater which used oil. A pipe went from this into the small bedroom, which also contained a chemical toilet in one corner, the pipe continued into the third room which had a sink, with no running water and a small table-top electric hob plate for cooking. We had to purchase water for all purposes by the barrel, and we were also able, at a later date, to get a small electric cooker with an oven.

This was our first home, and we set about making it presentable - some wedding presents out, photos, one or two ornaments, our bedding, our first meal! And a big portion of God's grace. I was content and was given the ability to 'make do' - to improvise. When sometime later we were given meat, chicken and bacon, a hole was dug and the joints we were going to use buried in the snow at the back door. Others were stored at the college. We also used the laundry and shower facilities. We felt blessed.

Then came studies and the very busy schedule of class devotions time - lectures - home study - exams - church services, every student was expected to attend every service - two on Sunday - Bible Class and Prayer Meeting. Later we had 'outreach', Billy in the choir, and he was used greatly singing solo - he had a beautiful rich bass/baritone voice and was anointed as he sang. I found my niche in children's work and was going with the 'Happy Hours' teams to neighbouring churches - often 30, 40, 60 miles away.

The honeymoon was over!

It was all so different - and we had to cope with living with each other - the honeymoon was over! Billy would take time and ponder things. I was apt to be hasty and impetuous. Billy - wait and see what happens! Doreen - need to know now! Billy, if stressed or asked to do something new, often withdrew into himself and would be quiet, didn't share how he felt. I like everything out in the open, and often added fuel to the situation by provocation. It was a learning process in more ways than one - God's word says "iron sharpens iron" Prov. 27:17, and we certainly sharpened each other. But God was with us - we were blessed and we were happy.

The money which Billy had when he first came to college now had to cover for us both. So we were reliant on God to help us to use it wisely and to supply our needs.

God often prompted Billy to 'give' to some student in real need. I had a lot to learn about this, but always, after debate, would back Billy's decision.

The Canadian people were very kind to all the foreign students. There were six Irish - four English - one American and a young girl from Jerusalem. All had been directed to Eston in a miraculous way, and like us had experienced God's intervention over provision - visas, etc. This had a bearing on later events.

The church members, and staff invited us to their homes for meals, gave rides in the cars if transport was needed. The first Christmas we were invited to travel with two of the boys and enjoy the festive season in their mum and dad's home. It was their way of serving the Lord. What a blessing they were - generous in their giving and their love. It helped me greatly in my first Christmas separated from family, and we had fun and laughter. Back in Eston we discovered a mistake. We had turned off the heater - the place was icy - the barrel of water froze, expanded, and joints opened - as it thawed it leaked. Oh, the joys of 30 below zero!

Chapter 7

Revival In College

In the new year, we foreigners detected a dryness - discovered that many students were second generation 'Pentecostals' and had not received the baptism of the Holy Spirit themselves. We grouped together, with the Dean's permission, for prayer between classes; we fasted by missing breakfast, and prayed before class devotions.

Visitation

In mid-February, a pastor came to teach on the gifts of the Holy Spirit, and the Spirit of God visited us in a spectacular way. The student body met for devotions as usual. One of the students was leading, there came a time when it went quiet. Then one student began to prophesy words to the effect that God was not pleased as there was tale-bearing in the body, and if the guilty person did not confess, they would be named.

I will never erase the images of that day from my mind. It was as if time stood still - then the head student got to his feet and with tears said it was him - he wanted to get favour with the Dean. He asked for his fellow students to forgive him. Such a presence in the room - no one moved

- no one spoke - no one went out - the only movement was staff coming in - they realised something was happening and wanted to be included. We were there from 8.45 - 3.45. The silence was intense - you hardly dared breathe - I personally was afraid the Holy Spirit would reveal some secret sin in me - but I was even more afraid that He wouldn't. Then someone would get up and ask someone else to forgive - perhaps a bad attitude. Even the staff asked forgiveness for allowing a student's behaviour to rub them the wrong way and they felt irritated. I had never experienced anything like this before, and as far as I can remember, only once since. One student had a recurring dream and shared it - one of the staff gave the interpretation which revealed something the girl had to put right. It was awesome. Towards the end, something beautiful - someone started to sing - in the Spirit - and almost instantaneously, one after another joined in until there was the most harmonious song. This was followed by an outpouring of joy. Every face was alight - students hugging students, staff hugging staff, staff hugging students - and now we were free to leave the building.

New challenges

Things returned to routine, but it all seemed easier after the Holy Spirit moving. And soon it would be end of term - exams over and marked. Ready for a three-day convention in the church with the graduation service for the third year students. Every one was excited about the summer. We had to vacate our home. Where would we go? What would we do? It must be what the Lord wants! So we sought His face. His Word to us was to trust, not to fear - we were set aside for Him - we were to just take one step at a time. So we packed our trunks - one to leave at college until next fall - one to go with us. People asked what we were doing. Reply: "We don't know but God does!" The first day of the convention a staff member arrived. Art Shepherd had taught personal evangelism for several weeks during the term and he came to visit us. Would we consider renting a basement in his home? But as he and family were often away in his evangelistic work we could have use of the whole house, look after his mail, etc., and he felt there could be work for Billy in the town. One problem - he wasn't returning home straight away - he could take our trunk, but the Lord would supply our transport. Oh, praise God, faithful to His Word.

Moose Jaw

Many people attended the convention including our Christmas-time hosts. They were also concerned about us and sought us out, were willing to have us at their home if we had nowhere to go. They were delighted with our news and offered to take us to Moose Jaw, if we didn't mind attending another conference they were going to in Saskatoon. We didn't mind! However, when we arrived it was fully booked - no accommodation. *But God* ... An elderly couple nearby became aware of our need and offered to share their motel room. They asked for a screen to divide the bedroom, and gave us a meal. The next morning they had a call which requested them to return home, and they said we could stay in the motel, it was paid for in advance, and they left their food.

Some days later we arrived in Moose Jaw. This was more like it - paved roads - plenty of shops, the bustle of a busy town. A beautiful air-conditioned home to live in.

Our host found a job for Billy to work as a nursing assistant with the mentally handicapped. He received two weeks training and as it was a government job it was well paid. It meant shift work. I hoped to get a job - I was an experienced comptometer operator, but no door opened. I was lonely, and I was afraid of thunder and lightning. As a child I had always fled to my parents bed, and even as an adult I needed some one else's assurance. Here it was different, because of the heat - electric storms were frequent, often without rain - the whole sky was lit up with a combination of sheet and forked lightning, the thunder-claps deafening. I had no one to run to but the Lord. He gave me comfort - gave me peace, and I came to the place where I could watch the display with enjoyment. Marvelling in the creation of the Lord - and I still can.

Billy came home from work emotionally exhausted. He was sensitive and the plights of these patients grieved him. He wept for them.

Used in the gifts

We got involved in the church. The Pastor was the one who taught "end-time truths" at Bible College. Soon Billy was singing and preaching, I was giving testimony - not just in the home church, other doors opened in the vicinity. Everywhere we ministered, God would use me in the vocal gifts, and I was surprised to read, looking back through my letters, how often after such an utterance the Spirit moved in the meeting. What a God we serve.

The Pastor had an office in the church and a secretary, who left to do a missions course, whereupon I was asked if I would like to help out. Would I ever! - But I can't type! Could I try? Yes - so I did - and seeing my typing efforts today, I wonder how I ever got his letters typed - but I did. I was also involved with all the paperwork for a daily vacation Bible school - in the planning - and ended up teaching children Bible truths. I could do it 'flexi-time', to fit in with ministry and Billy's work shifts. The experience gained here was invaluable to me in later days. Sometimes I took work home with me, and the deacon asked me to keep an account of the time I had worked. Later when it was time to move, I was given a cheque - a dollar for every hour worked, something I hadn't expected. God's favour.

The World Pentecostal Conference

We were also invited by another staff member from college to go with him, his wife and their two small children to attend the World Pentecostal Conference in Toronto in September 1958. We jumped at the chance. So we packed again, borrowed a tent, cooking utensils, sleeping bags etc., and off we set. We travelled by road north of the railway line through what was known as "stick country" - trees, bears. Other people we knew, including the College Principal, were travelling by minibus, and we often met up to eat. They took great delight in teasing the two foreign inexperienced campers - with pretend 'bears', spiders ... all wonderful good-natured fun, we soon were able to retaliate.

The conference was a once-in-a-lifetime experience, and we stayed near the Niagara Falls with friends of the Wilsons, the family who had invited us. We visited a peach farm, able to sample as much fruit as we wanted. We saw the Niagara Falls from viewpoints on both Canadian and American sides. We travelled back to Moose Jew via the USA, crossing the border south of our destination.

There were a couple of weeks before studies commenced, and the church had a visitor - an American preacher. We enjoyed his ministry immensely, and he seemed drawn to us - visited us at home, invited us out for a meal, encouraged us to share our testimony - this wasn't a hardship, as we were always ready and enthusiastic. Out of this came an invitation to Billy to consider joining him in ministry after graduation.

Mid-October saw us back in Eston. The little house wasn't ready for us, so we had a light housekeeping room until we could move in. Studies began in earnest my second year, Billy's third.

Another "happening"

Over the previous weeks my mum told us dad wasn't well. There was concern. I experienced another "happening". It will never be erased from my mind. I had a dream - I saw an uncle, whom I was especially close to, so clearly - he was distressed, and said, "Doreen, your dad is near death." I wakened, couldn't rouse Billy, so I climbed over him and went out to the living room and began to pray. In a little while Billy joined me. I took note of the exact time, and when mum's letter arrived we realised that at that precise moment, an ambulance was racing through Belfast, sirens blaring - my father had what appeared to be a heart attack and was dying. Subsequently we learnt it wasn't the heart itself, but a large gallstone pressing on something and stopping the blood flow. So he suffered the pain and symptoms of a real attack. This was only discovered after the family doctors suggested we should pray that the cause would be known. The student boy did, and a hospital doctor had the thought to x-ray other organs

- not just the heart. Dad had an operation to move the stone and had no further heart trouble. The stone was pickled and placed in a jar, my dad was pleased to relate the above account to friends.

Dancing in the Spirit

Christmas came around once more, and we were invited to stay with friends in Moose Jaw. Then in the New Year back to the intensive routine. About this time - and I'm hazy regarding time, but again very clear as to the event - once again we felt a dryness, especially in the church prayer meetings - always the same format, week after week. Again we got together to pray about this, and one evening the answer came! In the church prayer meeting an elder was again going through the usual procedure, when he suddenly announced, "If anyone wants to go and pray in the basement please go." All the foreigners got up and went downstairs - and others joined us, the Principal included, and the Holy Spirit moved. Some were weeping, some laughing, some just sitting quietly - some slain on the floor - three, including me, were singing and dancing to our own tune. I was told afterwards we danced over and around the slain without touching them. What a glorious experience - I had never danced in the Spirit before. We learned later that the staff yearned for such a move and it was their hearts' cry as well as ours. Again this move impacted the life of school and church, and when, a little later, a missionary came to visit, many students responded to his message by dedicating their lives to full time work for God. Looking back over the years, this was fulfilled - many of the friends became Pastors, Missionaries, or in evangelistic work. God is so good. His ways are past finding out.

Chapter 8

Back Home

Billy and I felt that God was directing us to go home and after prayer Billy felt to make a booking. By this time our money was almost gone. Because of the sterling block, our families could not send money even if they wanted to. Over the months they had sent food parcels, treats, Cadbury's chocolate, biscuits, Christmas cake, which was a great blessing to us.

So again, we looked to the Lord. I remember one devotion time - a brother called Art was leading - he said he felt to pray about money - "Anyone with a financial need, stand up." The whole student body arose. Prayer was made - promises in the word claimed. A few days later we experienced another 'occurrence'. We went to the bank to see what money was left and if we could use it for the deposit needed for the fare home. As we entered, the bank manager was crossing the room, saw us and said he was about to contact us. A cheque had arrived from the Bank of England. Apparently a mistake had been made in 1956 and they were now rectifying it. It was not just the deposit, but the full amount from Eston to Belfast. Glory! Glory! Glory!

Soon it was graduation time. Billy passed his exams. I didn't feel I should stay for my third year. I felt my calling would be fulfilled as Billy's helpmate in whatever ministry should open to us when we returned home. Our money lasted for food, etc., until school was over - the fare was paid, we still needed money for a sleeper - we ended up hiring pillows and just stayed in our seats on the train. The Principal had contacted friends in Montreal and arranged that we would be met and looked after. We stayed at their home, this brother took us sight-seeing during the two days before the ship sailed, and saw us safely on board.

After the graduation service the grad's lined up and everyone filed past to shake hands. I was very proud of my Billy and had eyes for him only, and I kept seeing him put his hand in his pocket again and again. The reason - people had dollar bills in their handshake. So God supplied our need for food on the train - for extras on the ship - for our need as we passed time in Liverpool before boarding the overnight ferry to Belfast. When we counted our loose change we had less than two pounds. From October 1957 to April 1959, all expenses had been paid, all needs met. What an accountant our God is!

Another chapter closed! What lies in store? How will we live? Where will we live?

Joyful reunion

It was with great joy we disembarked at the Belfast docks to be reunited with my beloved mum and dad. Uncles and aunts, Billy's cousins also there to welcome us home. Mum and dad opened their home to us, only too glad to look after us. Our first priority was to know God's will for service. John Wesley White had given us an address of an Elim Pastor in Belfast while we were at college. So he was visited, and on John's recommendation Billy was asked to minister. This opened up other contacts and soon we were visiting churches all over the country. I always went with Billy, taking part in the services - sometimes leading the meeting - sometimes just testimony - Billy singing and preaching. We had no transport, but dad came up tops - he would drive us. Mum came too - she loved the Pentecostal meetings. Dad never entered into the praise or worship - at least not outwardly - and had little to say. Sometimes George and Annie, Billy's cousins, came with us. Our income was ministry gifts - sometimes enough for just expenses, at other times to also meet our everyday needs.

House-hunting

It wasn't long before we felt the need to be in our own home, and so we went looking for a house. Mum liked us being with her, she didn't want us to leave. If we were determined to have our own place then let it be "round the corner" so she could be with us very frequently. We didn't see anything in the neighbourhood which was 'right'. Billy felt strongly we needed 'space' for ourselves.

Then, one day, we were returning home after a visit right across the city. Dad was driving and for some unknown reason, he turned off the main road and we saw a house for sale. Billy said, "Stop, we will look at it." The lady of the house was very obliging and showed us around. Billy and I immediately got the witness - this was our house! *And God ...!* With one of those coincidences - Billy received another unexpected legacy - enough to pay two-thirds of the price. My uncle was able to arrange a life insurance which covered the balance. Some furniture from Billy's mother's had been kept in friends attics for us, so we had that and received gifts. Four months after arriving home we moved into a semi-detached three-bedroomed house, bathroom, garden back and front. Mum and dad, George and Annie arrived with paint brushes, hammers, sewing machine - decorating, making curtains. Wonderful! God is so good. Even mum was happy for us - even though it was a good car ride or two bus journeys away.

Dependent on the Lord

So things settled down to a routine - Billy received more invitations in city area with Elim, Assemblies of God and many of the Independent Churches. We were still dependent on the ministry gifts - my words, Billy tried to instil into me that wasn't it, that we were dependent on the Lord, not the gifts. Sometimes it was tight. I remember one occasion when a bill needed paying, we had already looked in pockets and purses, but after prayer Billy had a strong urge to look in his suit pockets again, and on obeying he found a folded five pound note that hadn't been there before. On another occasion, an envelope was pushed through the letter box and was just the correct amount needed.

We did a lot of visiting - testifying, praying with folk - and had people to our home for the same reason. We were happy together, happy to serve the Lord. At times if Billy didn't have a meeting, he would 'go quiet', but we encouraged ourselves in the Lord. There was a lively A.O.G. Church about ten minutes walk away and we joined their meeting if not elsewhere. The Pastor asked Billy to preach and that opened further doors.

Chapter 9

Andrew

We spent Christmas with my parents for the family party. Soon it was a New Year. 1960 - Life went on, and in the springtime a baby was on the way. I still travelled with Billy, then in the summer he was asked to pastor a small Assembly in the city centre. How good God is - a regular wage, even though small, only one bus ride away, easier for me. We were rejoicing in our Lord. I was well - Andrew would be born in November. The Lord had spoken to Billy's spirit to say this child would be a boy and to name him Andrew - he would bring people to Jesus, just as Andrew in the Bible brought his brother Simon to the Messiah (John 1:40-41).

Six weeks before the expected birth, I was in the morning service, an elderly man came to me with a verse of scripture - Psalm 138:8 "The Lord will perfect that which concerns me." The next day the doctor discovered that my blood pressure was very high and I found myself in hospital for rest and observation. I was devastated - I was trusting God for health - why was I here? How would Billy cope? Then the verse came alive - "God would perfect" - perform - fulfil ...

As for Billy, he coped - or at least the neighbours did - they made him meals, washed, ironed his clothes, all except underpants - I found a pile when I got home - he hadn't liked to hand them over!

I don't remember a great deal about my hospital stay. I do know there were times I felt alone and afraid. The doctors decided to induce labour, and I was holding on to the promise. I had a long, hard day, but Andrew had a natural birth - pronounced perfect in every way. Within a few days I was home. All was not well, something had happened at the church, and Billy resigned. I cannot remember anything, and only know he resigned because it was in his diary. He was concerned about finance, with Andrew to care for. We sought God's will. I felt depressed. Christmas came, we were never in debt, and again we had Christmas with my parents. Andrew Hugh was the centre of attention.

Invitations and decisions

Another New Year arrived. Billy was approached by both the Elim and Assemblies, each inviting him to join their fellowship. Billy wanted God's direction and wouldn't make a snap decision. Then a church asked him to take their Sunday and Wednesday meetings. He agreed. It meant he had to travel a considerable distance to a county town. I wasn't able to go, so Andrew and I joined the local A.O.G. I started a children's meeting in my home. After prayer and research into the church organisations Billy decided he needed to join one, not be a 'loose canon'. He decided on A.O.G. - he felt their administration gave him more room to be led of the Lord. So he gave the chairman of the Belfast Council his answer, "Yes".

Around the Christmas period we had been given a gift and used it to buy carpet for the stairs and hall. It was laid down on the stairs and landing, but the remainder stayed in the corner of the hall. Billy had 'a feeling' it may be needed somewhere else - so don't cut it. I was exasperated.

In mid April, we had a visit from the A.O.G. Chairman. He told us of a church in Stranraer. The Pastor had left, membership had waned and it needed someone to bring restoration. Would Billy consider the job? I thought - no way - Billy said he would seek the Lord. We both prayed - together - then apart in different rooms asking God to speak to us, so we would be in agreement. We were to write down that we felt the Lord say. Both papers said "GO".

Stranraer

First of May, Billy and I went to Stranraer, sailing from Larne. My mum was looking after Andrew - he had progressed well and was a bonny baby. The A.O.G. Mission had three members, could give us £2 per week, and a free house - the manse - it consisted of a narrow hall leading to a narrow semi-spiral staircase. One bedroom, and a smaller room and old-fashioned flush toilet. Downstairs was the same. The main room smaller because of the hall and a small room leading off it. It had an old fashioned stone sink with a cold water tap. We came home - it was the Lord's will - and walked straight into family opposition - even mum, who was usually content to "leave it with the Lord", wasn't happy. How could I leave my lovely house? How could I? We were advised not to sell it, but to let it furnished. The rent would pay off what was owed. We got some second hand furniture packed up, and by June 10th the house was let - at least I had a good stair carpet! We moved in to my parents house once again until we set sail for Stranraer. They paid for Billy and I to have a week's holiday in Portrush - Andrew stayed with them.

In our hotel we got friendly with a couple from Scotland - guess where - Stranraer. So we talked, shared testimony, told them when we were due to arrive.

Sailing into the storm

July 4th came so quickly, again it was goodbye and off we sailed - into a storm - and although the ship berthed, no cargo could be taken off, so the container with our furniture, etc., stayed on board until the next day. God supplied all our needs - our new friends were on the quayside to welcome us, and took us to their house to spend the night. None of the three members were in a position to help.

Next day we moved in. I remember the wardrobe had to go in by the bedroom window - the frame was taken out - as the staircase was so narrow. We had no garden - the front door opened out on to the street. I thank God for His grace - this was the second time I'd left the comfort of a modern home, and had to 'make do'. I remember making a curtain to drape around two tea chests, propping a mirror on top to make a dressing table and somewhere to store clothes. We did get a small double bed in that room - thankfully as mum and dad came to visit us Friday p.m. to Monday a.m. each month.

I can't go into details, but we worked hard - started children's meetings, Sunday School and midweek, and made contacts with their parents. Little by little people joined us, some newly saved. God was undertaking for our needs. We showed T.L. Osborne and Oral Roberts films. It was a good time. Then something happened that disturbed us. We noticed that Andrew had stopped developing. He had a good single word vocabulary, was beginning to join words together, he was walking, interested in every thing - and now wouldn't speak - wouldn't respond. When I reported this at the routine visit to the clinic I was told I was being a fussy young mother. So prayer was made. Andrew was about 16 months old Although my dad came to our meetings, he was still resisting healing and water baptism. My mother was more on fire than ever and really concerned for dad. She was a woman of prayer and knew God's voice. We prayed over a handkerchief and she put it under dad's pillow. Billy counselled her not to nag him. On one of his visits to us he took ill, so in the early hours we sent for the doctor. The doctor was concerned, and said he would return in a few hours and if there was no change would send him to hospital.

Billy went into the bedroom alone, and prayed for him. We do not know what took place in those hours, and my dad never spoke about it. However, at breakfast time he was better, the doctor was surprised at the change when he came back. But that wasn't all. Billy was having a baptismal service that Sunday evening, and to our amazement and great delight - dad calmly said he wanted to be immersed in water. What victory!

Chapter 10

A Present Help ...

Another nine months passed - we worked hard - still didn't see any real improvement in Andrew - but the little church was blessed and flourishing. Billy felt he had taken it as far as he could go. Was this right? Was he to stay? Was he to go? Again, we sought God's face, and shortly afterwards Billy received an invitation to pastor an established church in Yorkshire. He went to visit the church, meet the people, and received an unanimous call. This answered a sign we had asked for so our decision was made to go.

Our people were sorry, but they also knew it was 'right', a new man was going to take our place. The date was set for our removal - and then a phone call, via a neighbour, would I ring my aunt as soon as possible. The outcome was to hear that mum and dad had been in a car accident - both ill in different hospitals. So we got ready as quickly as possible, and left for Belfast.

We had to let the removal men pack our things, and go to Elland. Billy then had to travel without me to the induction service. I stayed to nurse my dad and mum when they were discharged from hospital.

Some weeks later the doctors gave permission for my parents to fly to Leeds to stay in our new home, which I had not yet seen. We went by ambulance to the plane's door and again from the plane to our home. It was the most frightening experience I've ever had. Andrew was also afraid of the unknown, and it was hard to pacify him. He was heavy, and at three-and-a-half years old hard work. All the time my heart was calling out to my Lord, His grace was sufficient.

I remember how pleased Billy was to see us, he had tried so hard to get the house ready - photos, pictures, ornaments out, but never thought to unpack the blankets!

Settling in

Mum and dad returned home after a few weeks convalescence, and we settled in. The house was so much nicer than the previous manse, still no bathroom and the toilet outside. The church people were very supportive with Andrew, and we saw definite improvement, so much so, he was enrolled to start normal school when he was five, even though he still didn't speak much apart from some words. We still continued to take Andrew for prayer at various locations whenever we could, and we were expecting to see full recovery.

The New Year came around again and that spring we spent a day off in Huddersfield, booking tickets to go home (Belfast) for a holiday. I was expecting another baby, and I can recall clearly how elated we felt. Andrew was so much better and we were rejoicing, and that evening another blow fell.

Returning home that afternoon we have over a mile to walk from the bus to our house, and Billy had to slow down as he had tightness in his chest. When we got home, I discovered that I was beginning to haemorrhage. Billy ordered me to bed, saying he was all right would see to the tea and Andrew, etc. This was duly done and he came to bed - to awaken me a little later as he had severe pain in his chest and arm. We prayed, claiming God's word.

A little time went by and Billy asked me to call a doctor, so I went to the nearest call box. The doctor came at once, said Billy was having a heart attack, an ambulance was ordered and he stayed while I went next door to ask if my neighbour would look after Andrew. While I was out Billy told the doctor about me, so he wrote a letter asking the hospital to send me home in the ambulance. Billy was admitted to Halifax General very ill, the next 48 hours were critical. For some reason, no transport was there for me. Perhaps with my state of mind, I missed it, but I travelled back on public transport, phoned my parents, and they planned to come over on the night sailing with the car, as dad was still suffering the outcome of the accident. Mum had made a wonderful recovery, apart from her jaw which hadn't been set right, and she had special dentures to give her a 'bite'.

Anxieties and fears

The doctor came back to see me, and was very concerned. He said I wasn't to go up and down stairs, I was to bed rest - not an easy thing to do with a five-year-old who was very distressed. Andrew went around calling dada, and when he didn't come stopped speaking and began wetting himself. I was at the end of my tether. I can recall so clearly how I felt, the fear and anxiety about Billy. What will happen? What am I to do? No phone in the house.

Tears running down my face. I called out to God - "Help me, You're a present help in time of trouble." Sobbing, "Help me." Then into my mind as clear as if it had been spoken aloud, "Read Psalm 61." I reached for my bible and began to read. Verse 2 states, "When my heart is overwhelmed; lead me to the rock that is higher than I." I responded. "Lord, I am overwhelmed. Lead me. Lead me."

"I will trust"

Again, that voice, "Read on." So I did. Verse 4 "I will trust in the covert of Thy wings" - I will trust You Lord. "Read on" - Verse 6 "Thou will prolong the king's life." And I KNEW that Billy would live! And I experienced peace. A short time later, someone entered by the unlocked back door. It was a young woman and her husband from Huddersfield who attended our church. How did she know? They should be at work! But God had used the 'street gossip'. A lady who loved to be the first with news had seen Billy being taken in a stretcher in the ambulance and for some reason decided to go to Betty's house and tell her. God's ways are past finding out. I had help.

About noon next day, my parents arrived. I hadn't said anything about myself or Andrew over the phone, and they were so shocked. The doctor came back. His second visit that day and said I had lost so much blood, I was at risk and would lose the baby. I needed hospital. He would arrange to send me to Halifax to be near Billy instead of the usual one for my condition. So the ambulance again. I went on my own, both grandparents were needed to help Andrew as now both of his parents were out of the house. One of the ambulance men who had been the first time asked about my husband. I said I didn't know, so he went to enquire at the ward and told the sister I was being admitted. I asked him not to tell Billy. I knew he would live. I was taken to theatre. Next morning a nurse wheeled me down to Billy's ward - the sister had told him in advance - so we consoled each other. "God knows, we trust Him." They told me, it was a boy - he could not have survived. So to this day I carry the thought of our baby - a little David - in my heart. I think I was discharged later that day and arrived home the same time as a young lady from the Brighouse Church with a scripture verse to encourage my parents regarding me - Isaiah 55:8 "Thine health shall spring forth speedily." She was very surprised to see me, but then God has said "before you call I will answer" Isaiah 65:24.

Chapter 11

Billy's Healing

Billy was eventually discharged from hospital, very weak as he had damaged his heart and would need months to convalesce. Andrew was still very distressed - incontinent. No words - barely communicating. My parents returned home. The Christian community were wonderful. Ministers from different churches offered to preach and fill in for Billy. On a few occasions when there was a vacancy I would preach. I remember very clearly the reaction of one of our members (a man): "Well, I suppose if God could use a donkey He can use you ..."

In spite of our prayer Billy's condition wasn't improving, but we were believing God's word. Then one Sunday evening someone offered to take Billy by car to the service. He sat across the aisle from me - I had a 'special' little corner so Andrew could sit on the floor - Billy had no strength to sing. The doctors had said any extra effort could bring on another attack. At the close of the service the visiting preacher called on 'the Pastor' to close in prayer, and Billy stood up. In a weak voice he began to pray. Mid-sentence he moved into the aisle and began to run towards the pulpit. My first reaction - "Oh, he will die!" Simultaneously the Holy Spirit came upon the people and we all, as one man, stood to our feet and a great shout of praise went up. Billy ran back to his seat, and in a strong voice completed his prayer. He was healed. Within days he had taken up his ministry again. It wasn't until many years later we discovered that the scar on the heart was also gone.

He told me afterwards that God told him to run. He also felt fear, but said "If this is You God, I will obey." And obey he did.

More cause for concern

Andrew continued to be a source of concern. It was now apparent he could not start school. Doctors, specialists, etc., were divided as to his problem, and apart from being given a place in a special school some miles away we had no help. It meant waiting at a street corner for a bus to pick him up, and 'waiting' wasn't one of Andrew's strong points. He was becoming aggressive and would end up screaming. I am sure passers-by thought he had abusive parents.

Our hope was in the Lord. We prayed over him, we played Scripture in Song tapes. We took him to many healing meetings and men of God laid hands on him - if anything he grew worse. Now only wanting to kneel and rock back and fro. Church life went on, we were blessed with increase. The gifts of the Spirit flowed in the meetings. My parents came to stay as often as they could. Dad's neck injury and pain was worsening. My mum's jaw was a trouble to her. One Sunday morning a word of knowledge came from a member and she turned and pointed at my mum. Something 'clicked' in her face, her jaw was in line, but now her teeth weren't! When she returned home she had to have a complete new set.

In spite of all these happenings, my dad still didn't respond - wouldn't ask for prayer, kept aloof from the 'things of the Spirit'. I was happy in the Lord, working with children, Sunday School, Happy Hour, and because of the experience in Canada organised daily vacation Bible school in the holidays. Had permission from head teachers to hand out leaflets at the school gates. It was great - children got saved - joined the Sunday School - more contacts to parents. I remember the joy in the church. One lady 80 years old gave testimony how blessed she was to be part of it. She played the piano for me as I led. She went on to say "It was the only occasion I had to play between the keys!" In spite of my lack of tune, God blessed.

Missionary visitors

Billy always believed in the wider body, so we had many visitors - missionaries. If Billy felt it was 'right' and would benefit the believers, he had them minister. Some we met by 'accident', some were 'led' to call on us. One such person was Maxwell Whyte from Canada. They stayed in our home and had compassion for Andrew, encouraging us. Our home was good - the church had decided to improve it, and installed a bathroom.

So time went by. Towards the end of 1966 we received a letter from Maxwell Whyte. He had written, "Do not be afraid of pregnancy. You will have a healthy baby." A few days later I realised that I was already pregnant. How good is our Lord!

Some weeks later Billy said "Our baby will be a girl. God has spoken to me from Luke 2. We are to call her

Anna because she will be a prophetess." I had already thought if it was a girl to call her Rebecca after my mum. However, I had great respect for my husband's ability to hear from God so it was settled. In due time we would have a healthy baby, Anna.

Billy and I had a great relationship. We worked closely together sharing church work, visiting, etc., and he shared in the housework. We took turns to get up in the night for Andrew's needs. I never missed a meeting, taking Andrew with me. He seemed to be at peace in the house of the Lord.

Chapter 12

Anna

Soon the time came nearer to Anna's birth. My parents planned to visit us for a couple of months arriving some weeks before the expected event. This timing proved to be in God's will, as we will see later. My dad was in extreme pain, felt he could take no more, had been to see a consultant, who said the only option was surgery. Apparently his neck had been broken and never X-rayed at the time of his car accident and had set wrongly. They would try to alleviate the pain, but it was a fifty-fifty chance; if it went wrong he would be paralysed from the neck down. My dad said he would risk the op, to get free of pain, but asked to postpone it for three months so he could visit us and see the new grandchild. This was agreed, and he would come into hospital immediately after his return from England. He had some relief driving, walking jarred his neck. So they came. We were rejoicing in the Lord, praising Him for His word.

Ten days before the baby was due, a Monday, I attended the doctors for a routine check which alarmed our doctor. The baby was lodged with extended limbs and there was an added complication, never fully explained, but a danger to both baby and me. All efforts to turn the baby failed.

"All will be well"

I remember hurrying home to Billy, fear lurking, Billy's embrace, his support - "believe the promise". As our custom we went before the Lord, the church elders prayed for me Thursday evening. Next morning the doctor came to the house, he had cancelled the home confinement, had arranged an appointment for X-ray next day. I remember the sense I had, "I must confess to him that all would be well". I felt a tremendous sense to say it 'now' - don't wait until after the event, somehow it was connected to the scripture in Matthew 10 'Whoever confesses Me before men, him I will also confess before My Father who is in Heaven.' Other thoughts were invading my mind. "Think of Dr. McFarland, you're throwing his kindness and concern back in his face. What if you're wrong?" But God's word prevailed and I spoke up. "I hope for your sake that you're right" was his response.

In the early hours of Sunday I awakened from sleep with a sense of 'rightness' all was well, even though I had felt no movement within my body. I wakened Billy with my effort to stifle praise and tongues which bubbled up from within. I didn't want to waken Andrew, he didn't sleep well and once aroused would not go back to bed.

My mum was believing God, my dad didn't say a lot, but he was worried and concerned for his beloved daughter.

On Monday I attended early surgery as the doctor expected the X-ray result in the first mail and was distressed as it hadn't come. He decided to take me in his car to hospital as soon as his last patient was seen. He was worried as time was so short. I felt an urge to tell him of the night's experience, and he said he owed it to me to examine me, although any change was impossible! I will never forget the look on his face as he turned to my husband and cried, "She's right! She's right! The baby has turned and in the correct position for birth!" On Wednesday, 1st August, two days later, Anna was born at home with only the midwife in attendance. It was an easy delivery. The nurse never acknowledged it to me, but I overheard her telling a day-old baby, while combing a quiff of her black hair, she didn't know what had happened as there was nothing in her study book which could explain it!!!

Jubilation

There was great jubilation in our house. What a faithful God. His word cannot fail. The only shadow was concern for Andrew. He received a lot of love and attention, but didn't react in any way to the baby. He seemed to be locked in a world of his own. Yet hope was fired. If God could intervene in Anna's birth, He could help Andrew. My dad's relief was evident, but still no comment.

Sunday, 11th, saw us all in the morning service. Great praise rising from the people. At the close, Billy asked any sick who wanted to be anointed with oil (James 5) to come forward, and to our amazement and delight my father responded. After prayer he took off his special collar. We went home, elated, but once indoors pain poured through my father's neck. His arms fell limp to his side. Billy, undaunted, began to pray, binding the work of the enemy, encouraging my dad. We played tapes of T.L. Osborne, Oral Roberts, prayed again. Thanked God for the victory of Calvary, and several hours later, the pain left. Dad could move. How I miss Billy. How I long for the same audacity to be in me. In a few days, dad was out polishing his car.

Dr. McFarland called to see Anna and was amazed to see my dad with no collar, and this time dad gave his testimony. Hallelujah what a break through!

Victorious return

Soon it was time for them to return home. Billy instructed my dad to take no pills, etc., or pre med when he went to hospital, to ask to see the consultant first. He did, and received both an examination and X-ray. The consultant had the 'before' and 'after' evidence, wanted to know who dad had seen - what Quack! But dad gave God the glory with his story, and he was sent home. He had no further neck problem in the remainder of his life.

So life went on, routine services, visiting, broken sleep, tiredness. Then I had fibrosis. It was painful to lift a tea cup, never mind a wriggling baby and obstreperous little boy. We prayed and I was anointed, but pain and more pain, often in tears endeavouring to keep calm as Andrew was very sensitive to atmosphere. I tried a heat lamp, hot water bottles, various ointments - and just pain. Weeks later, again in church, a brother put his hand on my shoulder. He didn't know the need, but just said, "The Lord bless you," and I felt a penetrating heat go deep into my shoulder blade which lasted several hours and I was healed, set free from pain. Help comes from the Lord. He never fails.

Chapter 13

Questions & Answers

Another brother who was 'led' to our door was Brian Smithyman. Whoever called would be invited in for a meal. Billy was always alert to the need of discernment, and I was aware that both men were forming judgements and the unity of the Spirit was obvious. He was on his way to hold an evangelistic crusade in the area, and Billy committed to help.

Then we arranged to have a crusade in our church, announced it in our open-air services, leafleted the homes, prayed, all the usual preparation - and not one unsaved or stranger attended. The evangelist found God giving him a message for the church as Billy led, and the utterance of prophecy through me was in unity. I remember clearly on one occasion the very verse on Brian's notes was spoken out. It was awesome, the presence of the Holy Spirit was like a blanket over the whole congregation. Brian moved off the platform to pray for someone and before he reached the person he was slain and lay on the floor. One young woman ran out of the meeting, came back later to say she had gone to break off her engagement as her fiancé was not a Christian.

Andrew was present in these meetings. Anna in her pram. I believe this was to bear fruit for us in later years. After the crusade was over the sense of revival remained. Billy's heart was to be led by the Spirit, place Jesus Christ central, and so the meetings did not keep to the usual order. Sadly, this wasn't appreciated by everyone. "It was always done this way," was the cry. This was said by 'the elder' and many followed his lead, so Billy sought the Lord. He felt we couldn't keep the unity without compromising his beliefs. So we decided to 'put out a fleece' as an indication of guidance, and Billy made it known he was 'available'. If no response, we would stay, but we received an invitation to pastor a church in Radcliffe, and so we were packing up once again.

Crying out to Jesus

Around this time we had been given transport, neither of us could drive, so it was decided I would learn first as it would help getting the children home quickly, and Billy had to be last out of church. I hadn't passed the test, so a brother from Radcliffe came to drive the car back. I can't remember why I couldn't go with him, but I do remember the nightmare journey. Anna was eighteen months old, Andrew was nine and extremely fearful of noises, new surroundings, etc. Billy had to stay to oversee last-minute packing and removal men, and he would travel in their van. So here was I, boarding a train from Huddersfield, with a pushchair, a bag with necessary requirements, an inquisitive toddler, and Andrew screaming, seemingly rooted to the platform, refusing to step into the carriage.

Thank God for some helpful people. Someone grabbed my bag and chair, another Anna, and I lifted and heaved

Andrew on board. What emotions, embarrassment, anxiety, frustration, but a heart always crying out to Jesus. We were met at our destination by a church deacon, and he was so loving and reassuring as we were taken to his home for a meal. His wife saw to Anna's needs, she was a biddable child, unafraid of strangers, and I could prayerfully endeavour to bring peace to Andrew. As I write, my eyes fill with tears, as I get such a recall of these situations and I can 'feel' again how I felt at the time.

We were now pastoring a larger church, more responsibility. Billy made sure I wasn't squeezed into the expected norm of leading only women's meetings. He recognised my gifting to children's work's once again I was in Sunday School, mid-week children's 'Sunshine Corner'. It was in one of these meetings Anna, when 6 years old, gave her life to Jesus, and was most upset as the eldership wouldn't allow children under twelve to be baptised in water. We could only console her by explaining, Jesus knew she wanted to. We had Saturday night rallies, conferences, missionary conventions. Again all visiting personnel were 'put up' at the manse. It was a large old house, hard to keep warm. I passed my driving test, then Billy passed his. Andrew got a place in a very good special school with a very caring headmistress.

Looking for improvement

Life was hard for me, Billy continued to help as much as he could. Andrew was incontinent, I refused to keep him in nappies during the day while with me. I was prayerfully looking for improvement. So we had 'accidents' anywhere he happened to be - perhaps a door left open and in the lounge just minutes before an elders meeting! Wet nappies and sheets every night, broken sleep, Andrew would awaken and couldn't or wouldn't settle again, trying to quieten him so Billy and Anna would get rest. If Billy was free next morning he would get up to give me a break. We were the pastor and his wife, expected to 'be there' for everyone's needs. I have to be truthful, I was so tired I wasn't enjoying my 'quiet time', and would doze off. I felt resentment to Billy, even though I knew he did his best. I would punish him by not returning his embraces with the excuse I was too tired. But God is faithful and one old lady 'saw' the need. She offered to look after Andrew at her house, so Billy and I could go out together. Another family would take Anna home after the morning services, and another would take her to play with their children. Andrew loved 'auntie' Braham, he was at peace with her. She had lost her son at an early age, and told me she carried resentment for years towards God, but she said she found peace - "I've realised there are worse things than death."

Wise counsel

Anna started school, ten minutes walk up the road from home, a Church of England with a Christian vicar and teachers who loved the Lord. About this time Andrew's headmistress asked to see us both, and advised us to allow Andrew to go into a home for a week, so we could have a break. I resisted this - it was my responsibility, he wouldn't be happy, etc. However, with wisdom she continued to point out the benefits. I would get rest, be able to cope better, have quality time with Billy and Anna free of stress. She pointed out it would also be good for Andrew to learn to accept new situations, and should a crisis occur where there was enforced separation he would know he would go back home.

So we heeded her advice. Andrew was booked into Brookhall Hospital, and we booked a holiday flat at Fleetwood. We enjoyed our break. Anna revelled in having both mum and dad. It was soon over and we went to bring Andrew home.

We were met by a young doctor who surmised by Andrew's colour he could be a P.K.U. and took a sample blood test which confirmed the condition. He had written a letter which we were to give to our local G.P. We were given an appointment at Pendlebury Children's Hospital to see Dr. Kamrowen who had pioneered research into this condition. The doctor explained that P.K.U. stands for Phenylkestonuria. Phenylalanine is found in protein. The toxin is normally excreted by the pancreas, but this procedure was not functioning in Andrew's body. Therefore, the toxin built up and attacked the brain cells. Billy and I were devastated to realise that a blood test could have revealed this condition earlier. Especially when we learned that tests on all day-old babies started in 1960 - his birth year. He suggested Andrew should be put on a low protein diet, as his phenylalanine levels were very high.

Tantrums at tea-time

The next ten months were very difficult. Andrew reacted badly to the restricted diet. No dairy food at all, bread and biscuits were on prescription and were tasteless. He was only allowed a few ounces of potatoes per day. No sweets, chocolate, peas, baked beans or meats, only low protein vegetables and fruit. He had to take a glucose-based drink with the necessary nutrients in it. There were tantrums every mealtime, food was thrown! Anna was upset because of her brothers unhappiness. We were faced with a discipline problem. Anna could grow up with a 'chip on her shoulder', resenting her brother, or could be a spoilt undisciplined child. So, prayerfully, we disciplined them both as needed. Often taking Anna to another room, so as not to upset Andrew. As appropriate, he would receive a scold or a tap on his leg. Later when interviewed by Dr. Izmet at Greaves Hall Hospital, he told me I had achieved a lot by treating Andrew as a normal child.

The church work had to go on. Billy and I were both tired - Andrew's wet beds, disturbed nights, up early in the morning as Andrew didn't sleep, perhaps he was hungry. We were cross and irritable with each other and at times snapped at Anna. It was our faith which kept us sane, and a God-given ability not to allow resentment to settle, but to say sorry and to forgive each other on the spot, even asking Anna to forgive us. This was something else Dr. Izmet commented about. He said he knew of similar situations that had caused families to split up.

I questioned God

After suffering the diet for ten months there was further consultation with Dr. Kamrowen, and he decided the diet hadn't lowered the phenylalanine levels, and to continue wasn't worth the aggravation we were going through. He was very concerned about us, as this last prop was being taken away. I can't remember why Billy hadn't been able to attend, so I was on my own with Andrew, and replied I was a Christian and 'God's grace was sufficient'. He then said he had to be 'cruel to be kind' and explained that Andrew had extensive brain damage, so that the ceiling for improvement was very low. In fact I was not to expect any improvement at all!

I felt devastated - hit rock bottom, and for the first time questioned God, "Why? Lord ... Billy and I are serving You, we have made sacrifices. Why? Why? Why?" On my face before God, tears flowing, and again God spoke into my spirit. "You say 'My grace is sufficient', now prove it." Then the scripture came to mind 'that the trial of your faith being much more precious than of gold that perisheth, though it be tried with fire, might be found unto praise and glory at the appearing of Jesus Christ' 1 Pet. 1:7 (A.V.). I remember clearly my response. "Lord, if how I live my life with Andrew will bring glory to You, I will be satisfied," and again peace flooded through me. I am so thankful to the Almighty God, that submission to His will did not rob me of scriptural truth - God is the healer, by Jesus' stripes we were healed - nor of hope. I carry these twin concepts within my heart. Years later I came into the understanding of John 7:23 'Blessed is he who is not offended (caused to stumble) at me."

Setback

This proved to be a 'turning point'. At these times Billy would say very little, he knew both of us had to work it out before God as individuals, but he was always stalwart, quoting the word of God. So life continued, with renewed trust, strength and joy.

Then we experienced a further setback. Andrew's headmistress retired and the new head seemed to be more concerned for peace and quietness rather than encouraging the individual, and he considered Andrew disruptive. At times he was, but without consulting us the headmaster sought medical advice which resulted in Andrew being given Valium and Welldorm. We were not happy with this, but 'comply' or no help, and we needed help. Andrew was a full time job. I remain grateful to the saints, they tolerated Andrew's presence in the meetings, and we rarely missed a service. I entered into the worship as best I could and often experienced the Holy Spirit's enabling to bring forth a word of prophecy.

My parents were still visiting with us, couple of weeks at Christmas and three or four during the summer. On one of these visits my dad began to pass blood. He was very quick to ask for prayer and the bleeding stopped. However, when he got home it started again and he visited his doctor. The outcome - he was diagnosed having cancer of the bladder and hospitalised to have the bladder removed. We had prayer for him in churches all over UK and from missionaries abroad.

Dad didn't want to see anyone and literally turning his face to the wall, cried to God. God reminded him of King Hezekiah (2 Kings 20) and how his life was prolonged. My dad believed this was 'a word' for him. He went through terrible pain, passed 'blobs' in his urine for several days, insisting on another examination and the cancer was gone.

A wall of protection

The doctors had no explanation and sadly did not acknowledge a miracle, and although they ruled surgery out, transferred my father to Montgomery Hospital for 20+ radium treatments. I remember Billy was speaking at an Easter convention in London, and as soon as he could flew directly to Belfast to pray with my dad that a wall of protection would be around him. It was amazing, confounding patients, nursing staff and doctors. My dad suffered no side-effect whatsoever - no loss of appetite, no pain - it was miraculous. His one concern was for the other men receiving the same treatment who were so poorly. Dad witnessed to them, and I know one man kept in touch until he died. My dad lived a further eleven or twelve years completely free of cancer.

Chapter 14

Body Ministry

So life went on with all the ups and downs of pastoral work. Life and death, joy and sorrow. God was invading Billy's mind with revelation about the church of Jesus Christ, body ministry, not just a one-man band. He was very concerned that, although many were receiving the Holy Spirit, there was little teaching, and many were gathering in house groups without leadership. So again we sought the Lord's will for us. One or two of our church trustees weren't happy, I was with Billy when one said, "We pay you to do the job, so don't try to get others to do it for you." Billy felt it was the Lord's will for him to resign from A.O.G. and be free to respond to any group. We were invited to pastor a fellowship in Liverpool, and we both sought God's leading and both of us were absolutely sure it was the correct decision. The timing was perfect regarding our house in Belfast. Tenants left, we sold it quickly and we had the exact amount to purchase a house to suit our needs. Anna got a place in a good school nearby, and Andrew was transferred to a doctor in Olive Mount Hospital, also in the vicinity, and was to have a place in an adult training centre.

Billy was delighted. He had been asked to be the pastor, with a group to meet in our home. Another brother with his family, whom we knew and loved dearly, were also joining and he was to be co-worker with Billy. The person who 'planted' this group said we were to receive some financial support to offset expenses. So we settled in, getting to know people.

Andrew's new doctor decided we were not experiencing the 'real' Andrew, just a boy kept under with drugs. So he was taken off all. We felt this was answered prayer, but it added more pressure as Andrew had withdrawal symptoms. Our new home had an extra room so Anna could play, have friends in and not always putting up with music. The adult training centre was excellent. The married couple who were in charge were people after our own heart. They believed that no matter how low on the ladder a person was, there was always the possibility to go higher. Andrew wasn't kept in nappies whilst with them. Our thanksgiving intensified, hope arose, and Andrew began to respond. He began to communicate, touched himself, he needed the toilet, he began to reach out to others. This was often misunderstood because it was a pressure of fingers and if frustrated it was a real nip. Then came dry beds, the first in seventeen years.

The Lord uses people

Andrew's doctor decided we still needed a break, so Andrew would go into Olive Mount Hospital, but this was run as a 'home'. Individual houses, the staff were 'house parents' male and female, and Andrew continued to improve. Our wonderful Lord Jesus does perform miracles, but He also uses people and I am indebted to all those who were in Andrew's life in those three years while this was happening. It was very different within the fellowship.

I have never completely understood what happened, and I am aware that if you spoke to others you may hear a different account. It is not my heart to discredit anyone, but this is part of my story, and I need to be honest to how events affected me and how I perceived the situation. It's a bit like 'the chicken and the egg' - after the passing of years, I can't quite remember which event came first. I became aware that, although we had everyone's approval initially, there were those who desired a different leadership. The brother who was co-worker changed his view on 'end-time' interpretation. I also saw that Billy wouldn't endorse some ideas, as he didn't feel it was scriptural. Then 'they' decided another family had more 'need' of finance than our household, so our support was withdrawn, and the scripture given 'if anyone will not work, neither shall he eat', and Billy was told to find a job. This proved to be difficult, as he had been an electrician prior to 1956, and would require to be retrained.

I took my eyes off the Lord ...

Billy had been in the ministry full time since Bible School, and now, over twenty years later, was asked to find a job. He did, with Securicor. However, the driving, always against the clock, put pressure on him and an old injury from wrestling in his youth flared up, and his legs became painful. While this was happening, I developed a problem and was referred to a consultant. I did ask for prayer and received 'counselling' that God worked through medicine, etc. By the time I saw the consultant, the cysts had gone - I was healed, but I took his advice, because of Andrew and my age, to have a coil fitted. I lived to regret this decision - I felt I had taken my eyes off the Lord. The coil moved and was 'lost'. This meant I was admitted to hospital, underwent major surgery to search and locate it embedded in the bowel. I then contracted an infection in the wound, and had a serious reaction to the treatment given, and was ill for several days. Billy came to see me whenever possible between his shift work, he was devastated, trying to keep his own needs from me. Andrew was all right, he was in Olive Mount. Anna seemed to be coping, but who knows what goes on in a nine-year-old's mind?

Camp time

I was discharged from hospital to find the meetings had been transferred to another's leadership - very necessary in the circumstances. Then it was camp time. Sometime prior to this we befriended a young woman, invited her into our family circle, she was lonely - became 'auntie' to Andrew and Anna. She would often baby sit for us, and give the whole family the benefit of her love. She was going to camp with us, in our car, in our partitioned tent. She knew of Billy's painful legs, of my wound not yet fully closed, and in her usual helpful way helped us to pack the car and put up the tent.

We attended all the meetings, held in Harrogate, but because of pain and fatigue, we often lay down to rest, when others still fellowshipped together. I clearly remember, the picture is vivid in my mind's eye. One of the male members called Billy to join him and Billy was told he had no leadership qualities, he allowed a woman to do the work and was prepared to hide away instead of putting others before himself. Billy came back, withdrawn and near to tears. He was no longer in leadership, the old inferiority complex surfaced. He had failed God, the fellowship, me, the children. I had no answers. All I could hear from God was to the effect that He had put reins on us. I was able to appreciate the truth of that at a later date.

We had only been home a short time when Billy's leg was such a problem he had to give up work and he found himself in hospital undergoing surgery. We could not understand. All through the years we have experienced healing and even if delayed there was always a sense of well-being. This was different, it was as if the unity Billy and I enjoyed between us was being attacked. Then Billy was home, unable to drive for several months. No job, but we had sick pay. Andrew was easier to work with. Things got back to a semblance of normality. Then we had an addition to the family - a kitten.

A new friend

I had overheard Anna explain she was unable to have a pet because of her brother and I felt real pain. So Billy and I decided to give her a kitten. Andrew needed to be taught how to treat cats and overcome fear of the unknown. This little cat became ill and we lost him. Anna was distraught, and we were unable to get another kitten, so became owners of a beautiful tortoiseshell adult cat. She had a mind of her own, and seemed to deliberately choose to sit in front of Andrew with her back to him, tail moving, and she suffered the indignity several times of having it pulled. Until one day, she took the same position - Andrew responded, the cat was quicker, and Andrew had a scratched hand. From then on they had a healthy respect for each other. Andrew had learned another aspect of life.

One day we received a phone call from a very dear pastor friend, Peter Whiteside, asking how we were. He said the Lord had placed us on his heart. So Billy and I decided to go to his Saturday night 'rally' when Andrew was next due in Olive Mount, as we didn't have meetings of our own. So we went and were blessed and encouraged. The next day in our meeting it came up in conversation where we had been. I remember the silence, then the new elder spoke, "Now we know the reason for your misfortunes, you have gone from under our covering." This was the last straw. A depression settled over Billy. As for me, the Heaven seemed like brass, but we returned to Hesketh Bank to ask advice from our friend, which he gladly gave. "Come out, it's killing your ministry!" So we resigned. I had a feeling most people were glad. I was to receive a letter years later thanking Billy for his teaching and example of faith in God. It came too late for Billy, but did bring comfort to my heart.

The end of the tunnel ...

So, once again, change. Andrew stayed at Olive Mount each weekend. Billy, Anna and I travelled to Hesketh Bank for morning service, had a picnic lunch in Southport and sometimes attended the evening service together. We received a word of prophecy, something to the effect we were 'soon coming to the end of the tunnel'. Anna took this word to heart and would remind us of what was said when she realised her daddy was feeling low.

Gradually, new doors began to open, our pastor friend's doing, to follow up people who had come to the Lord in his tent crusades. We sought God's face eagerly, desiring to know His will for our lives, trying to discover the 'why's'. Then we were invited to a house group in

Southport which met midweek. Billy was to speak and, if 'auntie' could baby sit, I accompanied him. Billy began to regain his confidence, his song, his joy in the Lord. One thing we never lose was our love for the Lord and for each other. In spite of everything we were closer than before. Both of us had the witness in our spirits - we could be moving to Southport!

Our pastor friend put the suggestion to the Southport group that they would all seek the Lord, to see if it was His will that we should come and spearhead a move in Southport with the Fellowship as the basis. Four weeks later the couple of dozen or so were to report. With the exception of two, who were honest enough to say they didn't know, the rest were in accord. This confirmed what was already a fact in our thoughts. So our house was on the market, and we found a suitable one. The timing all came together, except we needed a further £1000, but we were given a gift for this amount, so we were able to buy the property with cash.

"Put God first"

We had two concerns, but our eyes were on the Lord. It was hard to take Andrew from the centre which was so helpful to him. His doctor in Olive Mount also practised in Greaves Hall Hospital, but there wasn't a similar centre. Anna had won a scholarship for a place in a Christian Girls' School in Liverpool and now we were moving - she was too young to travel. Some friends thought we were unwise, but Billy always wanted to 'put God first' believing everything else would work out ... God would undertake.

I did wonder why the Lord allowed Anna to go through the ordeal of sitting the exam, but this was used in her being placed in a different area from our new home. As one person in the education office told us 'off the cuff', "Your daughter needs a different standard from the nearby school, we have placed her in ... The only thing - seeing it is 'your choice' - you will not receive a grant for travelling expenses."

So Anna was in a girl's school, which up to September 1978 was the grammar school. The teachers, etc., had good discipline and moral standards, and our lovely daughter settled in well, soon making friends. Some from rich backgrounds - I often felt for Anna, as our home was so ordinary and in need of repair and decoration. How heartened I was when one of her friends declared she liked visiting us, it was a happy home. But I'm getting ahead of the account.

God's protection

My parents still visited us on a regular basis. Dad had retired, and they were tired of the tension in North Belfast. We never knew if it was political or because of their witness for Jesus Christ, but they only escaped their home catching fire because my dad 'just happened' to awake, visit the toilet and for some reason 'unknown' to him, looked out of the window to see the adjoining garage on fire. Thank God for His protection. The police said it had been deliberate, and if the fire brigade hadn't responded quickly the house would have gone up in smoke.

They put their house up for sale, hoping to move near us in Liverpool, but it had no buyers. As soon as we decided to move to Southport they had a buyer, and moved bag and baggage three weeks after us. One of our new friends in Southport was willing to store their furniture in a large garage. Talk about excitement, chaos, elation, frustration ... Looking back I wonder how I ever coped. But then we did, we drew strength from the Living God in the midst of the laughter and tears. Andrew missed these 'settling in' days as there was some infection in Olive Mount, and although it didn't touch his health, no one would go in or out until it was cleared, and he had to stay for nearly three months.

Chapter 15

Heartache and Tears

Excitement, chaos, elation, frustration - I think those same adjectives could be used to describe happenings in our new fellowship. It had been agreed it would carry on as a house fellowship as before and we would prayerfully decide how to expand the witness. But that was not to be.

Two weeks after we moved the husband and wife in whose home we met decided to withdraw their support. They said Billy had preached at another house group and therefore had no loyalty. In fact the only other place we had been was the home of a couple who attended the meetings and had invited us for supper.

We had thought this was friendliness and responded, to find that several other people were there and we were invited to give testimony - something which was always 'top priority'. I know to this day we didn't think of it as another hopeful house group, and there had been no ulterior motive on our part. The repercussion of this, in spite of the mother church and pastor's intervention, was that many people split and instead of the sound basis and financial support, we had only three or four who stayed true to the vision.

This had an effect on us as a family. We hadn't the money for house repairs and decoration. It caused much soul-searching. What had we done wrong? Had we missed the Lord? Billy became very quiet. I know I often provoked him. Added to this hurt and I suppose sense of rejection, things weren't good with Andrew. He had been given a place in the centre for handicapped patients, but it was obvious to us that the clients were more advanced than Andrew. He was expected to sit around a table with jigsaws, paints, etc., and he hadn't the concentration for this. So it resulted in disruptive behaviour. Consequently he had to leave and the only help was to attend Greaves Hall during the day and then, for regular breaks, throughout the year.

A time of pain

I can't begin to describe the heartache I experienced. I hated leaving Andrew in the noise, the smells and no training. What was the alternative? Had we done wrong by him? Andrew was now 18 years old, very strong physically, he showed his displeasure by nipping. At times my arms were black and blue. One thing was very apparent to us, the staff on the ward were very caring people. We pressed on, more and more dependent on the Lord. We never seemed to have money yet were never in debt. I remember when we had to fill in tax returns, praying over the forms that those concerned would believe that we lived on so little. Again, I had children's meetings held in a believer's home. This gave Billy contacts to visit parents and invite them to special meetings. It was a great joy to us when 'auntie' from Liverpool decided the Lord would have her join our fellowship. She found a place to live and because of Andrew decided to change course and become a nurse for the mentally handicapped.

We became very close. She was like the sister I never had. I remember one morning as I was about to drive off in our car, it was parked in a neighbours driveway to get it off the busy road - it set on fire. I turned off the ignition, jumped out and Billy, who had been at the door to wave me goodbye, rushed to phone the fire brigade. We stood with arms around each other calling on God to intervene as we knew if it blew it would damage our neighbours' windows, etc., and also passers-by on the road. We saw the flames from under the bonnet and the firemen arrived to put the fire out. Everything that was able to burn under the bonnet was gone. They didn't understand how it hadn't reached the petrol tank, especially as I had started the engine and the petrol would have been in the engine. We knew - God answered prayer.

God is our provider

Now we were without transport, needed not just for our personal needs, but to gather up the children. God is good. He is our provider. He uses people. A young man gave us a Ford Transit Van and the Hesketh Bank fellowship converted it into a mini bus.

So again we found a routine. Fellowship meetings in our home, children's meetings, attending the fellowship at Hesketh Bank on Sundays. Anna joined the young people's group and was being encouraged to play the guitar. Billy and I took turns to stay with Andrew. 'Auntie' helped out when she was off duty. Mum and dad bought a house about fifteen minutes walk from us and all was well - until September 1979, bank holiday Monday evening, and Billy had a coronary thrombosis. He was again very ill. Andrew had to remain on the ward so I could visit Billy and take the meetings. Our fellowship folk were very supportive. There was a lot of intercession on our behalf. Billy came home, had a time of convalescence and gradually got back into the work over the next few months.

Because he wasn't allowed to drive, it was decided Andrew would stay on the ward over the weekend. This proved to be helpful, not only to us, but to him as there was more variety in his life. He was able to be in our fellowship meetings and enjoyed the praise and worship, and again the people were very loving and understanding.

God's time

Over this time my mum's eyesight was deteriorating, and my dad was really concerned. Mum was a very determined lady, and if she decided to do something she did it. One day, early March 1980, dad was ill, and was admitted to hospital. Billy and I both felt it was God's time to take him home. My mother didn't and was very distressed, calling on the Lord to heal him. Dad pleaded with her to let things take their course as he was ready to depart. I was asked to take mum home, to allow my dad to rest. We had just reached home when we had a call to say he had passed away. I always regretted that no family member was with him. So many responsibilities. The trial of faith seemed never ending, but then being a Christian doesn't make us immune to the troubles that beset mankind, but it does give supernatural strength and grace to go through them.

Mum came to stay with us. The funeral was over and I had another problem. Mum seemed to expect me to take dad's place. She didn't want me out of her sight. Billy wasn't completely well, and I felt pulled between them. Loyalty to my husband and to mum. I must have leaned more to mum because I remember Anna telling me that it wasn't fair, I didn't walk beside daddy, I was always with gran. Billy didn't complain. We began to look for a larger house so mum could have an apartment of her own, and we could have space as a family. Mum didn't like this, if I didn't 'want' her, she would go back to her own house, and wouldn't be convinced it wasn't a matter of not wanting her.

Wretched

So back she went. Now I felt guilty - I went to see her every day, and she was always 'poorly'. I remember one time I put something in a saucepan to cook and needed to go and meet Billy. As I was leaving she said if she wasn't well enough, the house could burn down. I felt wretched. I couldn't stay, Billy would worry if I didn't turn up, that wouldn't be helpful for him. So I left. I felt so worried, I called at our doctor who said he would visit and took me back in his car. When we rang the bell, mum opened the door as right as rain, but was taken aback to see me. The doctor talked with her, took BP, etc., and she was all right. He said, because of her loss she was using a bit of emotional blackmail, so it cleared the air.

I was able to be firm, without being guilty and a good relationship was restored. Only my Saviour knows the tears and heart-searching that I went through, trying to be Christ-like. Even now writing the account, I feel disloyal, yet it was an ingredient in life. I loved my mother dearly and I know she loved me.

Chapter 16

Steps of Faith

The children's work grew, and we needed a larger place to meet. A Christian businessman had premises in the centre of the town, and he suggested we could rent the first floor. As was our custom this was put to our group for prayer, it was felt to be right. However, when Billy went to discuss rental details, he was told the business was moving elsewhere and we would have to rent the entire building or move. Again, to prayer - this would be a greater expense. Was it the Lord's will? Had we faith to trust Him? Again it was agreed to take the step of faith. There would be plenty of room for expansion, it would facilitate the vision for coffee bar outreach, Saturday evening meetings, etc. Again, the Hesketh Bank Fellowship were supportive, panelling the walls, putting in a kitchen and toilet, giving chairs and hymn books. This was exciting. The meetings were blessed, we had many visiting speakers all willing to give their time to see growth. There were never large numbers, but real quality and commitment.

Mum wanted to be in all the meetings, so she slept in our home Thursday and Saturday nights. Andrew was easier to work with. He and his gran had a lovely relationship. Things were a bit different with Anna. 'Gran' had accused her of taking a pair of 'granda's' trousers, so their relationship was strained. We knew she hadn't, but gran wasn't to be convinced. It was only with hindsight that I realise it was the early stages of dementia.

"Forgive my unbelief!"

There was a problem with the rent money. I think it was almost £400 each quarter - reasonable for the premises, but huge for us. It was often the eleventh hour before we had the cash. Billy was very strong in faith, and always maintained God would supply. Often my mum would step in with a handsome cheque. Then one day she announced that she was not going to give anymore. Nothing wrong with that. Several months passed and then the rent was due and it wasn't there. Billy spent time before the Lord and told me he was instructed to ask mum to help. I remember my reaction as if it was yesterday. "No way. You know what mum's like. If she says 'No', she means 'No'." Billy was adamant. God had told him. I was learning not to argue with that! "All I want," said my husband, "is for you to come with me while I ask her". So I did! I can envisage the scene. We walked up the path hand in hand - me nervous, Billy determined. Billy rang the bell, mum opened the door. Before either of us could speak she said, "I have been praying you would come. The Lord has told me I have to pay the rent this month!" Lord, forgive my unbelief. What a Lord we serve. What jubilation.

It was a busy time. Two services on Sunday, children each Monday, prayer hours two mornings a week. Our home group on Thursday evenings so Andrew could be included, Anna could also have sleep. Then the Saturday evenings. Billy was pleased, but had a deep yearning for a move of the Holy Spirit - more growth. There were times he went quiet, almost moody, I didn't like it, but then he probably didn't like my probing "Why? Why?" But then Billy wouldn't say so, where as I would! And still we grew closer together.

Andrew continued to cost us loss of sleep. Anna passed her 'O' Levels. She got a Saturday job with a good class cafe on Lord's Street. I remember her asking if she could go on the staff outing to Blackpool. Billy said "No, she is too young." He didn't know what type of evening it would be. A couple of days later, Billy was approached by a young man who introduced himself as the chef, and said if Anna was allowed to go he would see she came to no harm. Both Anna and I were taken by surprise when Billy gave his permission.

A lovely surprise

Time went by and we reached our Silver Wedding Anniversary. We had no plans to celebrate, money was scarce and more importantly, Hesketh Bank had a Bible Exhibition in a large tent, and we were committed to being there. 'Auntie' had asked us to have our evening meal with her. This happened frequently and we went straight from the tent. What a surprise! Anna and she had arranged a surprise party - friends from the fellowship, mum, cards, gifts and a cake. Billy and I were touched by the love which surrounded us.

We were both so grateful to our loving Heavenly Father who had kept us together for all these years - through joy, sorrow, fears and heartache. Kept us close to Himself. In spite of everything our love for each other had deepened. We were lovers, good friends, and bound up in each others lives. Another year went by. Andrew got very frustrated. I didn't know what was wrong. I don't know if he did, he couldn't let me know. On many occasions I had to call Billy from his study to pray with him, to calm him. He would quieten as Billy would hold him and speak the Name of Jesus over him.

Daddy's prayers

Billy had a wonderful relationship with Anna. If she was ill, or had a problem, it was daddy's prayers which worked. I remember on one occasion when she wanted to go somewhere that Billy didn't think was the right place for a Christian. So he didn't forbid her, but pointed out the pitfalls and then asked her to consider if prayerfully. Her reply was, "I haven't a chance! You will be praying about it!" And flounced out of the room. We learned later she talked it out with the youth leader and he gave the same counsel, and she made the decision to honour Christ. We were blessed with our daughter. Her sunny nature and love for her brother more than compensated us in times of difficulties.

Christmas came with all the extra activities. Billy underwent a full medical in the New Year for Insurance purposes to drive the minibus. He passed A1. Life was good, yet I was also aware that fear lurked in my mind. Billy was spending more and more time in prayer. We still prayed together, but this was his time with the Lord. Often he would encourage me to go to bed, he would follow shortly. I would awaken and Billy wasn't with me. Is he all right? I would creep downstairs, trying not to disturb

Andrew, get halfway down and sense the presence of the Lord. I wouldn't intrude, would stay on the stairs until I was cold, listening to Billy naming us one by one, family and fellowship, just caught up in the wonderful atmosphere. I would go back to bed, then Billy would come, and his arm would go around me and I was at peace.

Chapter 17

Billy Goes Home

The Sunday before Easter was a significant day. Billy announced he didn't have a word for the meeting, and he felt I was to share what I had on my heart. In the service I remember him saying, "Doreen and I have worked together for many years and she had never tried to usurp authority. I have asked her to speak this morning and she will be speaking into this fellowship a lot more in the coming days. You mark my words."

I felt uneasy. I didn't want that. I wanted just to support Billy as before. I knew many didn't like Billy's straight-forwardness, he would speak out even if it was a hard message. Perhaps I wouldn't and people would prefer the easier option.

On the Thursday at the house group, Billy was continuing his study of Hebrews 11, and if just happened to be verse 32 which mentions Barak. He went to the Old Testament scriptures and spoke of Deborah's role in encouraging Barak. I began to think - even though Deborah had such influence, it was only Barak mentioned in the New Testament list. It was as if a weight lifted off me, and I said, "Lord, I will be all the Deborah You want me to be, because at the end of the day Billy will get the credit."

The next day was Good Friday. We had a service, then a fellowship meal, with fun and games. Billy played footy with the young people for a time. Then he came to sit with his arm around me, just watching. On Saturdays we had a routine - Billy in his study, while I prepared food, etc., for the Sunday, doing household chores. But this Saturday, Billy asked me had I time to go for a walk. I will always be glad I did. So we went to the park, strolled hand in hand. Billy told me he was excited. He was on the verge of a breakthrough - tip toe with excitement. I thought he was speaking of the fellowship, we prayed for revival. It was a lovely time together.

Faith to carry on

The next day, Easter Sunday, Billy preached about the resurrection life and at the night, the four most important things - Jesus, His salvation, the Word and Heaven. He sang "When the roll is called up yonder I'll be there." The fellowship had some supper together and we went home. By the time Anna and mum were settled in bed if was after eleven when we went to our room. We talked about the good time over the weekend. Then Billy said to me, "Doreen, God is going to give you the faith to carry on this work. I can't go any further." I recall my reply. "Don't be silly, Billy! You've got faith." He just quietly replied, "You'll see!" Then he told me - showed me how much he loved me.

He had a table at his side of the bed with a lot of books on it - he was a bookworm. I wasn't looking in that direction, but I heard the books tumbling to the floor, and I said, "Would you like a hammer?" This was our humour, meaning he could make more noise if he had one. I heard no answering chuckle, and in that instant I knew he had gone. There was no warning, no cry, he just slid to the floor, knocking against the table. I phoned for an ambulance. The depot wasn't far away, they came very quickly. As I waited I stood looking at Billy and God spoke into my spirit. "I want you to take up the mantle and I will give you a double portion." I had only one response - "Yes, Lord." I asked one of the men to be with me as I told my mother and Anna. I rang Peter and Ida and they came as soon as they could. I had to go to hospital to identify the body. "Auntie" came to be with us. I will always think of it as "Easter Sunday", but in fact it was officially Monday 23rd, as it happened five minutes past midnight.

Then it was phone calls to my relatives - Billy's were already dead, mine were uncles and aunts, a couple of cousins - trying to cushion the news. Anna had arranged to work Easter Monday in the cafe, and I decided it would be better for her to be busy. With her consent, as she was about sixteen-and-a-half years old, I phoned the manager and he said she could work out of the public eye, and he would arrange someone to look after her, bringing her home if necessary. The person he chose was his chef, the young man Billy had trusted.

"Except a grain of wheat ..."

I thought a service in our home, Peter thought it would be better to hire the Chapel in the grave yard. He was right, it was full. I remember the scripture coming into my mind as we travelled behind the hearse, "Except a grain of wheat fall into the ground and die ..." I had left the service to Peter, and a retired Assemblies of God pastor who had joined our fellowship. Terry and Janice, friends from

Hesketh Bank, sang "Where the Roses Never Fade", and such a spirit of praise and joy, dancing came upon most of the people assembled, we never got to the message, it was time to vacate the Chapel. Ida said she had the real sense of Billy dancing before the Lord as he often did in the meetings.

"New grass will grow"

We walked in a procession behind the coffin to the non-conformists part of the cemetery and gathered around the grave. Once again the Spirit came with praise. Peter brought a word of prophecy - I didn't take in the beginning, but it left me with the sense that it was all right, God was in control. I did retain the end - "... The grass has been mown, so that the new grass will grow." I think this was Friday, 27th. On the Sunday Peter, from Hesketh Bank, took charge of both services. The following days I was very perturbed about the prophecy. I knew it was God speaking, but it wasn't clear. So I asked the Lord for clarification.

The second Sunday a friend of Billy's, who had been abroad and had missed the funeral, came to the service to encourage me and exhort us as a fellowship to go on with the work and vision for the Lighthouse, as we were called. He then prayed for me and went into prophecy, and I heard the exact words, "the grass has been mown so that the new grass will grow". Then he added, "... And you are that grass!"

Life had to go on. The Greaves Hall doctor advised me to let Andrew stay on the ward as extra night, so I could continue the children's meetings. I stepped into Billy's shoes, so to speak, and led all the services. I had Andrew home three afternoons and nights each midweek. Still had mum to visit, shop for and look after. Billy's death was a real blow for her to cope with. I can't begin to describe my pain. I knew I needed to praise the Lord in all circumstances, so I did, between sobs with tears streaming down my face. I felt I wanted to say sorry to all bereaved people I had tried to comfort in the past days, realising I hadn't known their sorrow.

Muddled thoughts

I tried to be strong for mum, Andrew and Anna. I feel I made a mistake with Anna - in trying to shield her I hid my grief. I realised later I should have been open with her, and we should have grieved together. In later years I needed to ask her forgiveness. Ever since his heart attack Billy had kept his weight down. I think I was angry it hadn't helped, so I ate cream cakes, etc., and my weight rocketed. I also had to deal with the thought, and even though I still don't fully understand, I know that in God's purposes it was 'right' for Billy to go home, and my ministry, work, whatever, would start in a different way. I felt guilty that it cost Billy.

My thoughts were muddled. How did the 'grain of wheat' fit in? A dear brother in the Lord gave me a little wooden plaque with the words, "As for God, His way is perfect." I had to accept that. I had to trust. I wrestled with the thoughts, "No one feels as bad as I do." I would remind myself countless others had lost their spouses, but they can't have loved each other as we did. And so it went on.

I had to deal with the fact that I had leant on Billy so much. Billy, what do you think? What shall I do about this? I had to transfer my dependency from him, and rely on the Lord Jesus. He became more and more real to me.

One thing I told the Lord was the fact I couldn't cope with last minute supply of rent money. Would He please bring it in earlier? - and He did. I was also blessed by receiving a widow's pension. Billy had been diligent to pay the self-employment stamp, and I also appreciated that he and I did our accounts together, so nothing was a mystery to me.

Chapter 18

My Maker, my Husband

Just two or three weeks after Billy's passing, Anna was due to sit her 'A' Levels, with her eye on a place in University. She had gained a year over her age group, and was a year younger than most of her classmates. Then she had severe pain and had to have emergency surgery. I was distraught. 'Daddy' was Anna's faith contact. He wasn't there. I felt useless, I felt I was letting my daughter down. I had no Billy to lean on. "God where are you?" Deep down I knew He was there for me! Anna came home to convalesce (bed rest) so I hired a tutor to help her with maths. I remember sending her in a taxi to sit her first exam. I didn't know what she was going through. Craig, the chef, came to visit her. He made a decision to accept Christ as Saviour ... but this is part of Anna's story. Perhaps it will be written at a later date. Suffice to say, she married him a couple of years later and the Lord undertook for all the wedding expenses. So Anna had 'her day' as she desired. The 'word' her dad received before she was born, is also coming to pass. She has a wonderful anointing to lead worship and many recognise that she has a prophetic ministry. What a faithful God I serve.

A few months after Billy's death, I attended Hesketh Bank's tent crusade held in Southport. Pastor Peter asked me to give testimony, my first time speaking in public outside my own fellowship. I remember a young man, the guest speaker, came to me and encouraged me greatly. He said that as I looked to the Lord He would open up the scriptures to me by revelation. I needed this! By now I was 'the speaker' in our fellowship two or three times a week.

Messages from heaven

I decided I wouldn't read any books, nor listen to tapes, just the Bible so I would receive the understanding firsthand. This must have lasted for a couple of years before I opened a book again. It is still a principle for me. I must have a 'message' or the understanding in my spirit first. I will then check it out with books and commentaries. I promised the Lord I would never make up a sermon. If it wasn't quickened to me, I wouldn't speak. In all the years since this has worked for me. In our fellowship if I hadn't the 'word', someone would arrive and I would have the witness to ask him to speak. It was always someone I knew. Billy had taught me to safeguard the sheep, don't open up the platform to the unknown. On occasions it happened that the Holy Spirit moved in a different way - perhaps worship was so rich, I didn't interrupt just because it was 'time' for a sermon.

My mum was needing more help. It was arranged she would attend a day centre for the elderly. Transport called for her in the morning and left her home late afternoon, either to her home or mine, depending on the day. So routine took over - housework, shopping, the fellowship,

Andrew's, mum's and Anna's needs. There were so many. 'Auntie' was so supportive. She came on holiday with me. I loved her like a sister. I praise the Lord for her. I missed Billy so much. At times the loneliness was unbearable. I realised the scripture which said, "Your maker is your husband" Isa 54:4 "... Your Redeemer the Holy One of Israel." It spoke to me, if the Redeemer of Israel could be my Redeemer, then He could be as a husband to me. So I began to trust the Lord for things Billy would do for me. If I had a physical pain I would say, "God, Billy would have laid hands on me. You're my husband, lay Your hand on me and I shall recover." If I didn't know what to do, I would say, "Billy would have advised me. Now You tell me." It was real, but even in this reality, I would often cry, "Oh God, I wish You had arms!"

Standing by the vision

Somewhere in this time, I experienced another setback. The brother who owned the lease on the building decided he wanted to sell it, and sent me a solicitor's letter asking me to vacate the premises. This was a blow! It would have been the easy option to comply. No one would have thought anything wrong, after all Billy was gone, I had Andrew and mum to look after, it was rather a lot for 'Doreen'. But something within me rose up. God had spoken. This building was for His work and I had to stand by the vision given to us. I didn't know how to respond to the letter and felt prompted to go and see a solicitor. I remember saying to her, "I am a Christian and it is not God's will I should take a brother to court. Please keep that in mind. But what can I do?" She told me the letter was out of order, as three months rent had just been accepted, and a further three months notice was needed. She replied to the brother stating this on my behalf. Praise the Lord - time for His intervention. Our little fellowship stood in agreement, praying the promises and the prophetic word through - others thought I was mad. Circumstances can show you God's will, "Go with it," was counsel I received from some folk. I felt I couldn't go back from the word given to us.

God's faithfulness

I remember in the weeks prior to the notice time, I showed the people from the wine bar over the premises, so they could measure up, etc., as they expected to have the place, and I told them I didn't think they would as it was meant for gospel work. I received strange looks. A few weeks later, Peter from Hesketh Bank phoned. The brother had contacted him. God had convicted him through a scripture about harassing a widow - I don't know the exact reference - but he had decided to give the lease to Hesketh Bank, so the Lighthouse could continue. What rejoicing! God is faithful to His word. How thankful I was to my precious husband, for his preaching, he always elevated the word. When I was sewing, knitting, Billy would read aloud to me. We discussed the word. We read books, sometimes I felt so tired I wasn't listening properly, but I guess the truth went into my inner man, and was there when needed.

I received a great deal of support. One such couple was an evangelist who we called 'Uncle Sam' and his wife. They shared in our meetings, gave advice. On one occasion Uncle Sam felt things were too much for me, especially with Andrew and mum. Mum was now registered blind, she had very limited sight. Uncle Sam said I should ask the Lord to send a family to help. I paid heed to this, it was always at the back of my mind. I remember one morning at our prayer meeting, sensing strongly that as a body we were to pray about this 'now'. It was amazing - the following week a family came to the Sunday morning service, they had just moved into town, and saw the service advertised in an old newspaper in a cupboard of their house. They came again and felt led to join. We got on so well. Billy had tried to teach me not to be impetuous, weigh things up, get the mind of the Lord. I was aware of all this, yet from day one we just seemed to flow together and everyone was blessed. It was now 1986, early spring. I felt eased, we were sharing ministry, the responsibility for the fellowship. The extra financial input was good. We got the ground floor up and running several days a week as a coffee shop open to the public, often being able to witness and offer prayer support. My heart was delighting in the Lord. I had help. I was able to take mum on holiday. She paid, so it was beneficial to us both.

Doors began opening for me to speak at Women's groups. I became a member of Women Aglow.

New problems, new fears

One afternoon when Andrew returned from Greaves Hall, he was very sick and vomited time and time again. I decided to drive him back to the ward as they were more able to care for him with a resident doctor who knew him. Four days later I got a call to say he was being transferred to an isolation ward in Fazackaley Hospital in Liverpool. He was very ill with food poisoning. The new family were wonderful, driving me down, praying and encouraging me. My special son, in an unknown environment, unknown faces. When I went to Greaves Hall it was to bring him home. My mind was full of doubts and questions. If he sees me will he want to come home? How will he react when he can't? How will I cope? How will ordinary, not mentally handicapped nurses cope? Oh Father God, you are a very present help in time of trouble. Be my help, uphold me ...

Another crisis, another deliverance

That first visit, Andrew was too ill to care. Oh Lord, heal him, I don't want to lose him. He was much better the next day and he had settled well, far better than my expectations, and I believe this was another step in Andrew's learning experience. It was several weeks before he was allowed home. He was the only person to be ill. I never understood how. He had been put back on a low protein diet, and apart from fruit and vegetables, the bread, biscuits, flour and vitamins were from a chemist. How grateful to God, my Heavenly Father. Another crisis and He sees me through. Another learning experience for me. The word of God, His word, can be trusted. It never fails.

About the same time I heard a report on the radio about Power of Attorney and felt the urge to enquire of a solicitor. This was a correct leading. Mum was glad to co-operate as she couldn't see to write.

A lady joined our fellowship and we were drawn together as prayer partners. This was so good, we met every week in our homes, encouraging one another. She had heard of Hollybush Camp and wanted to visit, inviting me to accompany her. It had been several years since I had been, and I was pleased to say yes. This was another significant time for me. Brother David Willows suggested that, now Billy was gone, I should consider joining the International Gospel Outreach. I met up with other ministers as well, and having prayed about this suggestion, decided that this was God's will for me, so I applied as a Christian worker on the basis of my involvement in the fellowship and was accepted. I have often thought, "What if I hadn't taken heed?" I didn't know at the time its influence on my future.

Chapter 19

Sorrows and Joys

I had already told my co-worker, again I don't want to use names so we'll call him J, that I would resign from leadership and was happy to sit under his sole leadership as Pastor. This seemed to be accepted by all. But within weeks he said he was considering leaving, and wouldn't say why until I came back from holiday. The week was booked, so I went with this on my mind, spoiling my peace and intruding into my thoughts.

After my return a meeting was called and J said he had been praying and considering why the fellowship hadn't grown numerically, and had come to the conclusion it was my fault. People wouldn't come because, he said, I was emotional in praise. He told me that what I thought was prophecy was actually manipulation, and what I considered the Holy Spirit was my own egoism. I know this wording is correct, I believe that for this book's sake the Holy Spirit has given me 'recall', but I also had it recorded in my diary of that year, August 1988. The troubles were not over. Three days later my dear friend 'Auntie' came to visit me, saying she had rejected me since Anna's wedding two years previously. I had no idea - I was devastated, hurt, bewildered, shaken to the core of my being. God, where are you? Have I been living in delusion? No. No. You have been too real to me in all my life.

Things were tense in the fellowship. I had so much pain! J carried on as if nothing happened. I couldn't pray or take part. I wanted to run and hide, yet didn't because of the testimony, wanted to safeguard other people's feelings. One thing was sure, I couldn't accept membership at I.G.O. I would withdraw my application.

Struggles and pain

Christmas came and I had invited the Fellowship for a meal on the Boxing Day. I made a full three course Christmas Dinner for about 20 people, and as we were washing up I slipped on the wet floor, fell heavily and broke my right wrist, and ended up in plaster for six weeks. It meant I couldn't help in the coffee shop - relief for all, and especially me. I was struggling with my feelings. I hurt so much on the inside, yet the others went about as if nothing had happened. I wanted to hit back, to retaliate, but the word of God restrained me.

I felt guilty that I had these feelings. Tried so hard to keep my emotions under control. Andrew was sensitive to atmospheres and could get disruptive. I was also trying to shield my mum, she had been in the meeting when the things were said and I knew she couldn't understand, she seemed to be very confused. I just didn't understand what was going on.

Two nurses, a man and his wife who worked at Greave Hall Hospital and had come to our meetings and to love Jesus, rallied around our family. Gordon would sit with Andrew whilst Pauline would take me shopping and help tidy my mum's house, etc. How I praise God for right people at the right time.

It came time to attend the I.G.O. Conference, and Pauline came as well. The plaster was off, but I couldn't drive. Mum and Andrew were in care so I could go. I needed the break, but I didn't know what to expect. I was withdrawing my application. Would I be able to worship the Lord? Would people think it was just Doreen, the flesh nature and not God's anointing? Would all my hurt, my inability to forgive, show? My wrist was sore and stiff - I felt miserable. But people old and new greeted me with love. At the first opportunity I spoke to David Greenow, the then president, and poured out the whole story. He wouldn't accept my resignation. He said he had known Billy and I long enough to know it wasn't true. He comforted me, advised me and prayed with me. My heart was warmed. I met Bob and Ann Searle, the administrators.

"Walk in your own anointing"

I met David Willows and asked him to pray for my wrist. I remember clearly he grabbed a young man who was passing by, asking him to join in prayer. Then David moved on, and the other person stayed. I had never seen him before. He said, "I believe God has a word for you", so I listened. "God is saying it is time for you to walk in your own anointing and not that of another." And he walked away. I had a witness it was God, but didn't understand. Billy had always given me freedom to be myself, to seek God for the anointing for the Sunday School work, so what did it mean? I went to my room and asked the Lord to speak again. I don't know if it was an audible voice, but I heard it in my head clearly. "You have functioned twenty-six years as Billy's wife, six years as Billy's widow. Now it is time to function in your own anointing." I knew a new chapter in my life was to begin. I knew I was to leave all the past, including the Lighthouse, and go into the future. I knew I would leave because it was God's will for me, and not because of my hurt. I knew God would enable me to forgive and forget.

Chapter 20

A New Start

I returned home, got in touch with Peter and Ida, they agreed with my decision and assured me of a welcome to 'come home' to the fellowship. It would have been easier for me to go to the local Elim, where I was in good standing, but I felt people might speculate why I should leave the Lighthouse and join somewhere nearby. I didn't want anyone to know what had happened. I wanted J to have the best opportunity to take the fellowship forward. I knew no one would think it strange for me to retire and return to the 'mother' fellowship.

J accepted my resignation, told me to go, and I felt real heartache. I didn't get the chance to speak to the children. I had birthed and nurtured that group, there were no "goodbyes", no "thank you's". "Oh Lord Jesus, help me to be Christ-like. I see in Your word I need to forgive as You forgave me. I can't, but You can. Do a work of grace in me." This was my cry for many days. I remember thinking I had forgiven, until one day, when walking with my daughter, I didn't want to go past the Lighthouse knowing it was open. Anna turned to me and said, "Mum, you are still carrying something in your heart. Have you truly forgiven and put the past behind you?" It was as if a knife pierced my heart. I needed to get home, fling myself on the mercy of God and have Him deal with any root still remaining. I know He did meet with me and I can write this account knowing I am free of all negative emotions. People say 'time is a great healer'. That is true, but the Holy Spirit is greater. He works so there is no bitterness, no revenge or ill feelings left, just the love of God which He places in our heart.

One of the congregation

He also gave me the ability to become 'just one of the congregation'. I had no 'hankering' to be in leadership. I did carry the feeling of rejection for a while, and the need to be reassured that I prayed or prophesied in the Spirit's anointing and not just 'fleshly'. I think this remains in me in some measure even now. I know the anointing, I know His voice, but I still have a tendency to ask someone if they had a witness it was of God. In one sense I'm glad I do, as I want to be right, and be open to correction, and not to be puffed up with my own ministry or importance.

So a page was turned, a new chapter began. Many things happened around the same time. Mum wasn't well, confused - perhaps the change had an effect on her. There were changes in Andrew's life also. He was moved to a new ward, Ward 20, on his weekend visits to the hospital. I was able to see this 'as all things working together for good'. Several months previously his normal ward closed and he was transferred to another. Whilst there he had the tip of his thumb and a piece of his ear lobe bitten off by another patient, he was unable to defend himself. I appealed to someone in authority and I was very thankful that

Andrew was moved very quickly. The personnel held a 'case history' meeting and I was invited to attend. I was shocked to hear that Andrew was regarded as P.K.U. with no expectation for improvement. The Andrew they knew was so different from the Andrew I knew. So I said so. I am so thankful my voice was heard and a Liaison Officer came to visit my home and observe Andrew's routine. She told me she was impressed. No wet floors, no wet beds, and Andrew 'helping' mum, etc. Changes were to be implemented on the ward. Andrew's bed was to be nearer the toilet and the staff were to encourage him to use it. He responded and a decision was made, he was capable to be considered for a place in the community when Greaves Hall was closed. Thus his new place on Ward 20. I shudder to think what would have been his future if these events hadn't taken place - but then I have a Heavenly Father who watches over me. He has promised to bless me and my children.

Balm to the wounded spirit

Something else happened which was a tremendous help to me. Hesketh Bank Fellowship had a Christian School using the A.C.E. system and I was asked if I would like to be a class 'monitor' or assistant. I would! so I did the necessary course and was in school two mornings per week hearing the children read, helping Sue, the teacher, with whatever she needed. What a balm to my wounded spirit to be with children once again. My God is so good.

I was also asked to help with a mothers and toddlers group - to bring a bible study to the mums as their children played. Little by little other doors for ministry opened for me at the fellowship. I am deeply grateful to Peter and his elders for all their trust and support. I was also greatly encouraged when a young man visited me at home presenting me with a bunch of flowers and thanked me for my input in his life whilst he had attended the Lighthouse.

Towards the end of the year I paid a visit to my friend 'Auntie', desiring to know how I had offended her. I was told the friendship was dead. I felt saddened. I was so fond of her, missed her friendship. I felt as if I had suffered another bereavement. But there was nothing I could do. It was also during this year, that I got the courage to visit my birth place, relatives and friends, without Billy. It was good for me - the welcome, the love that was so warm and real.

Concern

In some ways things were better, yet in others life was hard. Mum was unhappy. She said things were being stolen from her. I was unable to locate the brooches, etc., and yet had no understanding of what was happening. It wasn't until I was dismantling her home that the items were found ... neatly parcelled, a locket pinned inside the folds of curtains, something else pushed down the side of the settee. I found it all distressing. I was concerned about her.

Andrew wasn't sleeping well and I had disturbed nights. I would cling to God's word for strength and comfort. Found solace in prayer, especially with Esme, a prayer partner. I remember one occasion she said a verse from Joel 2 was quickened to her when praying for Andrew. "You shall eat in plenty and be satisfied." I didn't understand, Andrew was still on a very restricted low protein diet. But I had respect for Esme, and kept it on 'the back burner'. A few weeks later I had a visitor - Chris, one of the staff on Ward 20. He had been considering

Andrew's quality of life. He proposed, with my co-operation, to monitor Andrew's behaviour for a month, then take him off the diet and monitor him for a further month. Andrew would "eat in plenty". Christ was right, it would work. Another wonderful answer to prayer.

So the year ended. I made new friends in the fellowship, met up with friends from yesteryear. One was Marie from Huddersfield. She had been a member of the church we had pastored in Elland. She came to stay with me, to recoup after undergoing surgery for the removal of a cancerous growth. It was a happy time - a breath of fresh air.

I was still concerned about my mother, she was having 'little turns', perhaps just fleetingly. She said she was fed up with life. This was so uncharacteristic, as she had always been positive and full of faith.

A roller coaster

There was another problem - my house. It needed repairs. Things which we knew about when it had first been purchased had never been seen to - now it was chronic. I remember vividly how I went from room to room showing the Lord the damp patches, the loose banister rail, etc., and claiming His word. He would supply my need! I felt a peace. It would get done.

Life is like a roller coaster, full of ups and downs. Some good news, sometimes bad; and yet you get strength and grace to carry on. Good news, Andrew is to have a place in the community. Bad news, Marie's cancer has flared up and affected her liver. I speak to her on the phone, and I am shocked to learn she has so much fear. She loves the Lord Jesus as her Saviour, and this fear is robbing her of peace.

I hear the Lord 'speak' into my spirit that I am to visit Marie and prepare her for death. This is so contrary to my usual attitude to sickness. I usually feel the need to pray for healing, to pray the miraculous intervention of God into the situation, but I must be obedient, so I go and minister to her with the word of God. The assurance that belief in Christ means that death loses its sting. It becomes the gateway from this life into His presence - able to meet the Almighty God, because of sins forgiven when Christ died at Calvary. Then it was time to return home. I learned a couple of days later from a mutual friend, that Marie came into a place of joy. She arranged details of her funeral with her minister, asking that it would be a time of victory and thanksgiving. The nurses at the Hospice said she was so positive, and she passed peacefully into Heaven.

I was enriched by Marie's friendship. In more ways than one. I didn't know anything about her financial affairs, so it came as a complete surprise to learn she had left me some money. This was the answer to my prayer. I had no hesitation to use if for house repairs, not just 'make do' repairs, but new roof, kitchen, bathroom, etc. What a faithful God we serve. Praise His Name. My heart just swells with praise as I pen these words. It was not only the answer to my need, but it was the means of my son-in-law launching into his own business - but that's for Anna's story.

Chapter 21

God Does Have Arms

The months pass, life goes on, broken sleep, concern for the future days. Could I cope with Andrew and mum if she is unable to be in her own home? Am I being selfish? Was that the reason she wasn't already living with me? Need answers, guidance from the Lord. I had a lovely holiday with a new friend, Jean Holt, from the fellowship. We went on a coach tour and there was a lot of laughter, just the tonic I needed. Again, Andrew and mum were in care, and I was free to enjoy the break.

Soon after returning home I had a phone call from the lady in charge at the day centre mum attended. She felt mum had a personality change over the past days, she was concerned about her going to my own home. My reply was without hesitation that she should be brought to me. I called the doctor, who next day brought a consultant to see her. He said she had a severe T.I.A. (Transient Ischaemic Attack) and would probably have more, each one would do a little more damage to the brain, and he said she was also suffering from dementia, which accounted for all the delusions about 'they', thefts, etc. So mum moved in. I dismantled Billy's study, gave away books and some of my furniture so that mum could have her own furniture around her, anything to ease her hurt of leaving her home. I loved my mum dearly. I wanted to fulfil a promise given to dad that I would care for her, but it was hard. I had to resign from Women Aglow. I was still able to keep speaking engagements in the day time while Andrew and mum were in day care. Andrew stayed at Greaves Hall on weekends, but mum was with me. I felt so frustrated. She didn't want me out of her sight. She didn't want me to read. I should be talking to her. She didn't want TV as she couldn't see. "Oh God, help me. I want to be Christ-like, I want to serve You. I'm tired. You have promised strength to those who wait on You. I haven't even time to wait on You."

I remember lying in bed, listening for Andrew in the next room, mum in the room below, and thinking if either one has a problem what do I do with the other. I cried before the Lord and had to rest in His word. He would be there for me - and He was.

Helping hands

Craig and Anna were helpful. I could ring them. Neighbours across the street said to ring them, and God raised up another couple to befriend me - Keith and Jill. They invited me and mum to their house, they visited me, sat with mum. They brought so much fun and laughter into my days. I can never express how grateful I am to them. Jesus does have arms - His people. This was also manifested through I.G.O.

One morning I received a phone call from Bob Searle who asked if I would be free in about three weeks time. My thoughts went into forward gear ... did he want someone to stay at my home? "No, no!" was the reply. "I.G.O are having a holiday in Austria and someone has paid for you to go, you will only need some pocket money." I was stunned. I had never experienced anything like this. What emotions, elation. Praise to my Father. Then the practical thoughts kicked in. I don't like the heat. What about mum and Andrew? I need to give at least two months notice for the social workers to apply for respite care and I plunged into disappointment. I won't be able to go. I phoned Anna at work to tell her and received a rebuke. "Mum, don't you think that God who has provided you with this holiday is capable of sorting all these things out? Trust Him!" And she rang off.

"Oh Lord, I am sorry. Please forgive me. Cleanse me from unbelief. Show me Your power. Tell me what to do now." I felt prompted to ring the social workers. Their reaction was the same. "Wonderful, you need the break. We will work something out. Tell your friend you will be going."

Time of refreshment

It was great. Mum was allowed to stay at the home where she had day care. Andrew was at Greaves Hall. Craig and Anna drove me to Bob and Ann's home to stay overnight. The fellowship - the love - from people whom I had not met before, was a balm to me. There were meetings each evening - singing, praising, testimony, always the word of God. What a time of refreshment. It was also a very definite milestone - I realised for the first time I could survive in high temperatures, and even more importantly I realised God didn't mind a lot of money being spent for my pleasure - after all He had provided it!! I returned home uplifted, encouraged, rested physically. I needed all I received. Mum got more confused and was unable to dress herself properly. I needed to be in two places at once, both she and Andrew had to be washed and dressed and ready for their lifts to day-care. I got through each day. My friends were telling me it was time to consider having mum in a nursing home, but I couldn't. I loved her. I had promised dad!

A prayer partner

The year ended, the New Year began. What would it bring? January 18th Craig and Anna were involved in an accident. Another car ran into them and Anna had severe whiplash. I was now needed to help her with housework, heavy shopping, even cooking. Andrew was moved into the community. I hadn't realised it would be full time. I had thought it would be as in Greaves Hall. However, my Heavenly Father prepared my heart in advance, He spoke through another new friend. Stella attended Hesketh Bank but moved to live in Southport, and as I passed near to her home, I suggested we could travel together.

This was the start of a friendship - a prayer partnership. One evening in the course of a conversation she said, "Doreen, have you ever thought that lads of Andrew's age have left home, and got their own place?" It was a strange thing to say. She knew about Andrew's mental handicap. But it stayed in my mind. Once again I had a visit from Chris the ward manager. He told me that in order for Andrew to receive all the moneys, grants, etc., he would need to reside at the Community House full time. This would be Andrew's home. I could visit him and he could visit me.

I had one concern. I wouldn't be able to pray with him, nor would he have fellowship with believers. *But God ...!* How many times do we read those two words in the scripture? God had it in hand. I could trust our Saviour to look after him. I knew without a doubt that Andrew's spirit responded to the Spirit of God. I have to admit I was taken by surprise the way it happened. Chris said he recognised Andrew would be cared for physically and financially, but he had spiritual needs and he was prepared to take Andrew to church - to the fellowship I attended. The Lord never fails. He does abundantly above all you ask or even think.

Words of prophecy

I was able to attend the I.G.O. Conference at Swanwick and was given a word of prophecy. God had a ministry for me. I would have a voice and now was a learning time until it was 'time'. My head was full of praise. God was in control. I was not 'left on the shelf'. There was a future for me in His service. This was especially good to hear as I had a scripture in my heart regarding the call of God on my life. This had been affirmed many times and I was 'waiting', sometimes disheartened because I seemed to be less in 'ministry' than ever before. Now I could wait patiently knowing 'the now' was also ordained of God. Truly all things work together for good to those who are called. Hallelujah!

Some weeks went by. Mum had another T.I.A. - more severe. She came around before the doctor arrived and told me not to worry. She is in Jesus' hands. I recorded in my diary ... "I thank God for lack of fear." It was around this time I received further encouragement. Stella was in my home. We chatted, discussed the word and prayed together.

119

Mum and Andrew were both in bed and we were undisturbed. Stella had a prophecy and again it seemed to speak the same truth of the scripture I held. One word was different, and I didn't know its meaning. So I looked it up in the dictionary - it meant the same as the word I'd had. The Lord had again confirmed His word to me. He always speaks in the mouth of two or three witnesses. I didn't feel free to share this with others, so like Mary I kept all these sayings in my heart.

A witness to my Jewish neighbours

By May I felt exhausted yet again. I don't understand why prayer seems unanswered. My mum had stood firm for healing and health for forty years, and now was unable to grasp her own need. I am so thankful that it is the Lord who keeps us. We cannot keep ourselves. In spite of my 'feelings' something must have been seen because my Jewish neighbour remarked about my strength and cheerfulness. "If we were going through what's happened to you, we wouldn't be smiling!" I remember answering him, "It's not always smiles. I have tears but if you see anything in my life it is because of Jesus whom I believe is your promised Messiah. And in Him I trust. He is my refuge, my strength." Nothing more was said, but I received an opened door and had the joy of witnessing about Jesus from the Old Testament scriptures many times over the next few years.

By now Mum was tired in the early evening and wanted to be in bed, but by the early hours was up trying to get dressed ... Mistaking the armchair for the commode! I try to pacify her and not awaken Andrew. I still went to school, still helped Anna, and it was a constant cry with God. Then help arrived. I had a home help each weekday to get mum bathed, dressed, washing in the washer and ironing done. Praise the Lord. She had another T.I.A. and went to hospital. What was I to do? Does she come home? She recovered quickly and was sent home, so it was out of my hands decision-wise at this time.

Hidden in the rock

Stella had another word for me. "You are hidden in the rock". This reminded me of an incident some years earlier. Billy and I supported a Hesketh Bank tent crusade at Preston, the speaker had a word "for the woman in the green coat" (that was me). "You will have many troubles, but the Lord had His hand on you - you are in the cleft of the rock." When these confirmations come you don't know whether to laugh or cry. Even now, I feel the emotion. God has been so real, so close to me. Tears prick my eyes once again, but a joy rises from within.

Stella came again. She was a source of strength. She took a day off work to accompany me to a church where I was to speak. She said I was encouraging her, she felt she was being discipled. She had another word, "You are insulated. All the problems will not affect you, it will be like water off a duck's back". I still have the little duck she bought me to remind me of Gods promise.

I needed it. I had the hassle of selling mum's house. Another sale had fallen through. Then I was informed there would be no transport for Andrew. That meant I had to keep him happy, until mum's bus came for her, then drive him to Greaves Hall. An entry in my diary reads "I'm standing on Psalm 34". Some days later I wrote "Mum doesn't know me. I sent Andrew by taxi. He behaved badly and the taxi man won't take him again. I'm clinging to Your word Lord. Psalm 84." I claimed the call on my life which I believed God gave me through Jeremiah chapter 1. Perhaps this is the time to share it. With my hope and dreams, without being presumptuous.

The God of NOW!

I had been reading the word, seeking God's presence and I felt a compulsion to read Jeremiah 1. Several verses seemed to stand out and I had a distinct sense it was personal to me. Some things I could accept easily, especially the first part of verse 5 ... "Before I formed you in the womb I knew you, before you were born I sanctified you" - well yes, or at least from I was three months old when mum made a promise to give me to God's service. The more I thought about this the more I understood God's ways. He is the eternal God, the God of NOW - always NOW. He has a plan for each life. The truth dawned in my spirit. It was God all the time - the events at my birth, mums vow was instrumental in the beginning process. That meant I could accept the "I ordained you ..." It was God's plan and He made the appointment. I stalled at the next word " ... a prophet to the nations". I kept that simmering on the back boiler.

I read on. In verse 7 I felt the Lord was telling me not to make an excuse I was to go to wherever He would send me and He would tell me - command me - what to speak. At first glance this wasn't too bad, I was already learning only to preach what God would quicken in my spirit. But meditating deeper, I realised - if an excuse could be made - perhaps it would be a more difficult place to go. The next verse seemed to underline that ... "Don't be afraid of their faces". Not everyone would be happy with the message God was giving. Then reassurance - God, the Lord, would be with me. "Read on", was the prompting, and I knew from past experience to obey, so I did. "Behold, I have put My words in your mouth ... set you over nations and over kingdoms. To root out, pull down, destroy, to throw down to build and to plant. I knew God was speaking to me. I think I felt a little of how Mary felt when she said, "How can this be?" Yet I knew God enough to know if it was God it would happen. I had a lot to think about.

A calling confirmed

Some time later I was drawn back to this chapter and all the verses were emphasised in the same manner as before with the addition of verse 17. I was to "prepare myself and arise - to speak and not be afraid before their faces". I felt there was a warning in the next sentence, "lest I dismay you before them", followed by a promise, "I have made you ... a fortified city and an iron pillar." As I have already said, over and over this 'calling' has been confirmed. When Stella had prophesied, the words had been "God has made you as a strong plinth through your circumstances". The dictionary states that a plinth is the "lower square member of the base of a column" - base supporting. I came to the place where I accepted all that was 'spoken' to me - and believed it would come about - even the bit about 'prophet'. If God had ordained this, then I would be, by His grace. I would not get in the way with fear and unbelief.

Chapter 22

Fly Like An Eagle

I look back over the last ten years with absolute wonder. I can trace God's hand in guidance, in opening doors, in discipline, and I feel overwhelmed with His faithfulness.

But I'm getting ahead - I go back to the happening of 1992. Mum was so disturbed in the night that I purchased a baby alarm for her room so I could be alerted early. Good idea, except I hear every sigh - and I don't get much sleep, always on the alert. In October I noted a change in mum's breathing. I rushed down to her room only to find she was having yet another T.I.A. - this one was very severe. She was taken to hospital. This time I had to listen to family friends, doctors and nurses and make arrangements for mum to go to a nursing home. Anna and I prayed for God's guidance, and she was given a room in a home with staff trained for her special needs, it was about a mile from my home. God is so good. To my surprise she settled in very well and we had good quality time together. I was able to take her out in the car, wheel her in a chair, have a coffee with her.

So another year ended and a new year began. Andrew moved into his new home. Now I had a different problem.

I was on my own. I heard noises, jumped up, and no one was there. Again I needed to be more dependent on the Lord. He opened up the scriptures on prayer to me. I have written in my diary, "Lord I feel so humbled." I was not sure what I meant then, but I know what I mean now. The more you get into God's word, the more you realise you don't know it. The closer you get to the Lord, the more you realise you need to be even closer. In these times with the Lord I felt I wasn't to just start to go places or take up work. I stopped - but to wait and allow God to open doors.

A sparrow ... or an eagle?

Once again it was I.G.O. Conference time. A time of encouragement. I was asked to give a testimony. Bob prayed for 'a door to be opened', another brother prophesied "You will be used in intercession - you think you are a sparrow, God will cause you to fly like an eagle'. This was balm to me. I was still carrying consequence of rejection. I needed the reassurance that it was God's spirit and not just Doreen. It's amazing how you can feel so sure at one time and yet the enemy can fire 'an arrow' right to the most vulnerable spot. Andrew was brought to the service at Hesketh Bank - Chris and he sat with me. I was so thankful, and at the same time felt a little hurt. Andrew related to Chris and not to me. This was something I needed to get over. He needed to 'grow up'. He needed to be 'cut from his mum's apron strings', but he was my little boy - a special boy. God trusted me with Andrew and his needs. Now our Lord was opening a new door - a good future for Andrew, and for me.

What a joy it was a few weeks later to see another carer commit his life to Jesus. Praise God, Andrew was bringing people to the Lord, even though he couldn't talk. Life was full of ups and downs. I heard a rumour that the Lighthouse was closing. Even though it was right for me to leave, I just couldn't forget the prophetic word that that place was to be used for the work of God. Still, I couldn't do anything, it wasn't my responsibility now. A few weeks later, I received a phone call from Peter. He wondered what I would think if the Elim Church would use the building. I was pleased on two counts, first, that he asked my opinion, and secondly, it didn't matter to me who carried on the witness, so long as it was still going on. So Peter was ready to give the lease over to the Elim pastor.

Tears of joy

A couple of months passed, and one day I remember I had visitors in my home. I hadn't intended going to any evening service, but I had a very distinct impression I was to attend the one in the nearby Elim. It was so strong, I explained to my guests, and went. I had never met their Pastor, but was greeted warmly by several people I knew. One lady asked if I could be free Wednesday of the coming week and I replied that I was sorry, but it was 'prayer night'. The service began and a gentleman was asked to give a report of their outreach. He began to say how they had received the lease of the Lighthouse - how God had supplied the money to refurbish the coffee bar, and a lounge, so people could received professional counselling from a spiritual basis. Then he said, this vision could not have happened if it had not been for the faithfulness of Billy & Doreen Moore. By this time the tears of joy were running down my face. I was saying in my heart, "O Lord, how great You are. You didn't need to let me hear this but You have, and I am so grateful." The gentleman went on to announce there would be a service of dedication the following Wednesday. I had a sense I had been too hasty in declaring I was busy that night, but what was done was done! The service ended, and as I was about to leave a lady I knew grasped my arm and said she wanted me to meet their Pastor. She introduced me and he said, "Doreen of the Lighthouse ... I've wanted to get in touch with you. I would like you to come to the dedication. I feel the testimony of how it started is necessary. Please come." This time I knew enough to accept!! I walked home as if treading on air. How good is my God. What a balm to my heart. How glad I was to have allowed God's grace to reign and forgiveness to take place in me.

Truly blessed

It was truly a blessed Wednesday evening. The vision God gave to Billy and I was the same as these dear saints had received. I still have the letter in my possession that the pastor wrote giving details of his vision. What God declares, He will do. It is only us human beings that can thwart His plans, but God will use some other obedient heart.

Around this time I joined a team from I.G.O. to go to Guernsey for a holiday convention. Bob & Anne Searle were the leaders. We relaxed during the day and held services in one of the local churches. The aim - to encourage the believers. It was a joy for me to share testimony at one of these services.

In June I had a bad chesty cold. I felt poorly, but was still needed to do Anna's housework. As was my custom, I asked the elders to pray for me and I slowly recovered.

One evening I was awakened by a phone call from the Nursing Home at 2.50 a.m. Mum was passing blood and was being taken to hospital. I hurried to get dressed and drove to be with her, calling out to my Saviour. She reacted badly to the doctors. She only needed Jesus. She pulled out the drip, tearing her hand. He confusion intensified. She was taken for several tests, some weren't successful because of her resistance. She was eighty-eight years old, desiring to go home and be with the Lord. I cried out to God to intervene. Then the report of the blood test was given to me. Mum had a form of cancer - inflammation 15 cm in her rectum. The doctors were determined to investigate.

Agreement in prayer

I got another early phone call. Mum had fallen out of bed. She may have broken her nose. Again I hurried to be with her, and I was heartbroken to see her bruised face. I laid hands on her and claimed God's word. Next day I was told her nose wasn't broken. I didn't feel I could burden Anna with the cancer report. I went to Peter and we agreed together in prayer that she would receive a healing touch and be spared surgery. Then I was asked to sign a consent form on mum's behalf. I was in a dilemma - if I signed I was going against mum's wishes. I could only go by the past. She had always trusted God and had received many miracles in her body. I felt that was why she had resisted the doctors. On the other hand, if I didn't sign, I could be in trouble with the authorities. I was due to see the doctor the next day. I remember going home, crying out to my Lord for guidance for His will. I felt to go and talk to the staff at the Nursing Home, and they felt mum would feel more secure with them until her hospital examination came up. They were willing to nurse her, they would telephone the hospital and suggest this. And it happened. Mum was released from hospital on the strict condition if she worsened before the recall, she would be sent back. Somehow I wasn't called to see the doctor. My precious mother never had any further haemorrhaging and was never recalled to hospital. Once again, God undertook. He never, never fails.

God's dealings, our dealings

In the midst of all this trauma, God was also dealing with me - my attitude, etc. Stella drew me aside and told me I had spoken very curtly to another friend. I wanted to make excuses - I was tense - but "Jesus never answered back". So I had to swallow the desire to justify myself and go and apologise. I couldn't hear God's voice and obey when it suited me. I had to learn to be right in all my dealings.

Mum recovered enough to be able to go out in a wheelchair. I took her to the local store and she held the basket on her knees and was thrilled to help me. She loved having coffee and chocolate biscuits in the cafe. I wheeled her to visit Andrew at his home, and the staff there made a fuss of her. She was happy. I was happy.

Chapter 23

Testimony Time

During August I received an invitation to visit friends in Northern Ireland, and felt confident to leave mum, Andrew and Anna in God's care. I needed the break. It was a great time to renew fellowship and be able to share with them the goodness of God. To be able to share the gospel message with someone I had not seen since the war years when we had been evacuated to the country as our home was bombed.

Conference time again, and I was greatly challenged by the testimony of a church who held meetings for old people. I shared this at Hesketh Bank and was invited by the elders to start a team to visit Old People's Homes. This I did, and we went into six different Nursing Homes, one a week, and also visited mum's home on a Sunday afternoon. Singing the good old hymns, testifying to God's love and proclaiming the simple gospel message. I believe God's spirit ministers to man's spirit, even when at times it seemed their mental ability was gone. Staff often remarked how they were easier to work with after our visit. Many who couldn't hold a conversation, and some who didn't speak, would join in singing the words. We had one lady, Jean

Holt, especially picked for our team, who would ask God to whom she should go to talk to at the end of the service, and it caused great joy when she led many to accept Jesus as their Saviour. Others, who were in their right mind, had depended on being church members, or because they sang with the choir had never realised they needed a personal Saviour, and responded, believing God's word, and had assurance of sins forgiven and hope of heaven.

Mum's testimony

The next 'down' - I was told the doctor thought Andrew had diabetes. I asked Pastor Peter to pray for him when he attended the service. A few weeks later I received news - the second blood test showed he was clear. Praise the Lord. That's good. Then I got another early hour call - mum had fallen and had been taken to casualty. I arrived as she was wheeled in from the ambulance. Nothing broken, but her face was cut and bruised. The nurse was to clean it up. Mum began to speak, "I'm trusting Jesus", and she began to recite the twenty-third Psalm. The nurse stood listening with a bowl of water in one hand and a swab in the other. Mum finished, sighed and then allowed the nurse to attend to her. I took the opportunity to explain that mum was a Christian and what a Christian was.

Another statement in my diary read, "I am at my wits end!" Andrew was passing blood. The family doctor said he would have to see a specialist, and he had been hoping to avoid that. The carer with Andrew was pressing for an appointment to be made. I asked for time so Andrew could receive prayer. The doctor granted my wish. I think he had seen enough divine intervention to humour me. The next day, I received a call from Andrew's carer. Andrew was really poorly. I contacted Hesketh Bank and asked for prayer. I had an appointment to preach - Oh God, I need You. Give me strength. He did. I spoke from Psalm 112 - The established heart does not fear. I wrote in my diary, "I'm standing on the promise of Zechariah 9:12 ... Return to the stronghold you prisoners of hope. Even today I declare that I will restore double to you." Lord, I believe, help my unbelief. Bring me up to the standard of Your word. I took the little duck in my hand. All this worry would not harm me - it would be like water off a duck's back. By the 23rd Andrew was back to health - no blood - and none since.

"I need wheels!"

Another year ended and a new year was ushered in. It wasn't many days old before I experienced another trial of faith - my car was stolen. I was attending a bible study in a house group situated in a busy main road on the outskirts of Southport. I parked in front of the house, close to a car in front and another car drew in behind me. I was careful to put on the wheel lock, check doors were locked, enjoyed the study and came out with key in hand - no car. I experienced something new. My initial sense was not shock or fear, but peace and I heard myself saying, "Praise the Lord. Let's see what He does for me this time." I was taken to the police station to make the report, and then home. I told the Lord, "I need wheels", and because of my commitments to school, etc., I really did.

Next morning I contacted my mechanic who looked after my cars for repairs, etc., and he just happened to have a car, which I could buy quite cheaply. This I did, and he advised me to look for a better one if mine wasn't found and I could easily sell this small car. The stolen car was never found. The Insurance Company sent someone to my home. Satisfied it had been a straightforward theft, they were quick with the paperwork. In the meantime a friend told me of a Ford Sierra for sale and stated the price which was £100 more than the Insurance. The company asked if I was happy with their offer and I answered "No" as I needed to purchase this Sierra, and they gave me the extra money. The "new" to me car was all I wanted, which included a radio cassette player. I really believe the Holy Spirit dropped a gift of faith into my spirit which enabled me to trust God, and know that I knew my Heavenly Father would undertake.

God's marvellous ways

I still had the smaller car to sell, and was disappointed when people who viewed it didn't buy. Then I heard that Peter & Ida's daughter and husband were coming from Alabama as Peter had suffered a severe stroke. Terry & Janice were good friends of mine and I heard the Lord prompting me to lend them the car. This I did, and it answered their need for transport whilst in the U.K. They returned the car on the eve of flying home. I advertised in the paper once again and I had a buyer. God's ways are marvellous.

During the car episode, mum had fallen on several occasions. She seemed to be covered in bruises all the time. When asked why she tried to run she replied "I had to catch the train - I've to meet Hugh". She was back in her mind to her courting days. The staff explained that these flash-backs of memory were so real, she thought it was really happening.

My mind was so busy - how can things go so well on one count (the car) while the problems for mum were ongoing? I tried to get the thoughts for the meeting where I was to speak. I'd written in my diary ... "So many thoughts I feel like yelling to my head, 'Shut up!', and the scripture came - Be still and know that I am God." The scripture is life, and what I couldn't achieve for myself, the word of God brought peace and as I meditated I realised afresh that God was at work in the midst of chaos and activity, and He would bring about His will.

The blessing of I.G.O.

Bob & Ann Searle, the adminstrators of I.G.O., had moved to North Wales with the I.G.O. Office. They had Saturday conferences each month. I felt it was within driving distance and attended when I could. It was so good, so uplifting, that I invited Bill & Stella. They, too, were encouraged and so each month we went. Others saw how blessed we were and they went the next time.

Bob & Ann opened a Bible bookshop in Penmaenmawr, and wanted to expand by having a coffee bar. I was sure they didn't need my help, but at the time I offered and they graciously allowed me to 'help'. I believe with hindsight this was ordained of God, and part of His ongoing plan for me. Once the coffee bar was running, I did see a real need for voluntary helpers, and I offered to travel from Southport (86 miles away) to spend one day manning the shop. Bob asked if I could make it Thursday and stay overnight so I could be part of the prayer meeting. I agreed to this - it wasn't a school day. After I had gone many times, I felt it was time to resign for the school work. This I did, and I was released with blessing, as all concerned could see my heart was towards North Wales because of the I.G.O. outreach.

It was in one of these prayer meetings I met a brother from Northern Ireland. He was a great blessing when I had to attend my uncle's funeral in Belfast, meeting my plane and driving me to the service. God has so many ways to supply our needs. I have stated this already - He uses people! Oh that we would hear His voice and be quick to do His bidding. This brother, Billy, moved to Bala and invited me to speak at one of the meetings.

I remember clearly the day I was to drive from Southport. I was doing some shopping and I fell heavily, hurting my knee. The security officer in the arcade wanted to send for an ambulance, but I declined and hobbled back to the car. Every step agony, every breath a prayer ... "Oh Jesus." It eased slightly but I dreaded having to put my foot on the clutch. But I arrived safely. I could hardly greet my friend because of pain and he realised something was amiss. When told, he prayed for me, and, praise the Lord, I was able to stand that evening to preach the word, with only a tenderness if the knee was touched. Billy later moved to South Wales to pastor a church there, and I have been on many occasions to minister. He met a lovely lady, they are now married, and I praise God for their friendship to me. To be in God's family is so wonderful.

On the see-saw

By the time September came mum had had so many falls. She had a black out - she recovered - she fell again - needed an X-ray - no broken bones - she was well for days - then another fall. Up and down, up and down. I was on an emotional see-saw. Was I right going to Penmaenmawr?

What if I was needed - it took at least two hours to drive home. "Lord I do believe I am in Your will! Lord, take mum home! Oh Lord, am I selfish? Have I a right motive? Do it for my sake or hers, I'm asking!"

Keep praising the Lord!

Then I received word that Andrew had cut his head and had been taken to casualty! What was going on? Mum, Andrew, Anna all under attack. This wasn't God - God is a good God. I pleaded the blood of Jesus - by His stripes we were healed. I could only rest in the Lord - not easy - but I'm thankful He gave me the ability to hold fast - to know what was His will for me - not to be sidetracked - not to get involved in a self-pity party - but rather to keep praising Him. My beloved husband used to sing, "When the skies above are grey, keep praising the Lord." This really worked. It did something within. It released joy which was not dependent on circumstances, but sprung from Jesus Christ. 27th September mum fell - had a T.I.A. - recovered. On the 28th a friend and I were booked for the I.G.O. Conference in Swanwick. I decided not to cancel and trust God with mum. I got home on the 30th and she had been O.K. Why could it happen for a few days and not all the time? Did I not believe?

In October, Bob invited me to speak at his church, the Oasis in Penmaenmawr. Brother David Greenow had a word for me. He saw a light cloud over me, and I would be guided by the Lord. I would know when and where to go. How good God is. He knows my heart searchings and reassured me.

Chapter 24

Ministry Doors

The last Saturday in October was Rally Day at Penmaenmawr, and I felt a great compulsion to ask Anna to go with me. I knew David Hathaway was the guest speaker and he prayed with the sick. Anna agreed to come with me on the condition that if she was in pain I would turn back. I have written the account in my diary. We left her home at 11 a.m. The traffic was heavy. Anna wasn't so good. We went through the Wallasey tunnel to find we had to take a detour, which wasn't easy to follow. I was trying to drive smoothly. I could see Anna was tense. We got on to the A55, stopped at a MacDonalds - just over halfway, with another forty miles to go. Anna couldn't take the pain, was in tears, panicking - wanted to be home, dreaded the journey.

I wrote in my diary ... 'I began to realise something good was to happen, and the devil knew and wished to hinder us.' I was praying inwardly. I felt we needed to be at the meeting, yet I couldn't break my promise to Anna. I left her in the car to phone Bob, praying that God would undertake. Bob agreed that Anna should come and promised to pray to that end. I remember saying, "Lord it will have to be You." When I got back to the car, Anna had changed her mind. She would go on.

I remember how I felt, driving at the full 70 miles per hour feeling nervous. I wasn't all that experienced at that speed. Praying Anna's condition wouldn't worsen, and feeling very relieved to arrive safely. Bob had asked David to pray with Anna before the meeting began and her pain eased. At the end of the meeting he prayed with her again, and she received words of encouragement. This was the beginning of real hope for her, but that is her story. I tell this much because of the effect these events had on me. I hurt because she was my daughter. I wanted to see her well. It stretched me to the utmost. I was forever pulled between 'my feelings' and the promises in God's word. "O thank God - He wins. I can be victorious through Him."

Pulled to Wales

The staff at mum's home were concerned for her safety. She needed twenty-four hour supervision which was not possible. She always was a determined lady, and with the dementia that trait was heightened. They asked for my permission and the doctors to put sides on her bed. This didn't work, she tried to climb out over them, and had another fall. So it was decided not to have the rails, it wasn't so far to fall from the bed. The year ended and I felt the pull to North Wales and the work there.

Another New Year. Where does time go? I had an established routine. Visit mum each day I was at home, visit Andrew once a week, do Anna's cleaning and shopping, take her for treatment, travel to Penmaenmawr. Then new doors opened. I was asked to have teaching input, working with two other I.G.O. Ministers - Kingsley

Armstrong with his residential "Joshua Course" and John Levy and his "Nehemiah Bible School". God had been dealing with me and opening up His word regarding prayer. The I.G.O. Trustees had invited me to be the prayer co-ordinator for the I.G.O. Fellowship. So prayer became my subject.

As I responded to these opportunities, the situation changed with mum. She became quiet, didn't or couldn't walk much. This was better in one way - she couldn't hurt herself - but not in other ways. She was more frail, didn't know what was going on. Sometimes she didn't know me. One day as I sat holding her hand and talking, she said, "Oh dear, dear. Doreen hasn't come". I answered, "She has. I'm Doreen." "Oh no you're not. My Doreen was a lovely little girl." I felt as if I'd lost my mum, and it hurt. God's word states, 'Cast your care upon the Lord for He cares for you.' "Lord I do give You my concerns." It's hard when you hurt for those you love, when you see them in pain ... Anna's whiplash, Andrew's handicap, and now mum. "Lord, don't just carry my care, carry me." He did. I got rest, peace, strength and an ability each day to praise Him, not to be offended or stumble, but to carry on.

Alabama

It was in the midst of these circumstances I received another challenge. This was a good one. Would I go to Alabama to visit Terry & Janice? Ida was going, but wanted a companion. I prayed about this, talked with Anna, also with Bob & Ann. They confirmed to me I was making the right decision to go. So again I was trusting my Lord Jesus with my loved ones. I knew I wouldn't be able to get home quickly, but again I had peace. I knew I had made the right decision. Friends said they would visit mum. What an experience. I had never been on such a large aircraft, not for such a long flight. I was excited, and I enjoyed the whole experience. It was wonderful to see Terry & Janice, and their home, and to visit a large Pentecostal Church in Montgomery.

Prison ministry

Terry & Janice, his sister Lily and her husband Brian had a prison ministry. Ida and I were invited to accompany them on one visit. It was an eerie feeling to go through the gates - to have cameras, purses, etc. taken from you - the Bible searched in case anything was hidden. We were not to wear white - the inmates had white uniforms and if a head count was needed, it could cause confusion. More gates - doors to go through all locked behind us. There was a small building used as a chapel. Inmates were allowed to attend, Prison Officers with them. These women were lifers, many had killed! I experienced something wonderful - God's grace! Some came forward to greet Ida and I, thanking us for coming. I could feel their love and love in me for them. These were my sisters, we were all saved, our sins forgiven - their murderous deeds, my self-righteousness. What a joy it was to preach God's word. Ida and I were both asked to share. What a joy to worship the Lord with these precious people. Others came to get away from boredom, but the Holy Spirit could reach them also.

Terry and Janice had been married for eighteen years, and had been holding on to a promise given them from God's word, that they would have children. They were faithful in prayer, claiming the promise, and Janice was pregnant. God is faithful and again it was sheer joy to rejoice with them, to add my petition for a safe delivery. How it encouraged my heart to hold on - to keep believing for promises given to me - not to allow wavering or unbelief to abort the hope of their fulfilment.

I had two full weeks, then time to return home. I travelled back by myself as Ida was staying longer. Again I enjoyed the flight, was relaxed, refreshed, and so, so thankful. My Saviour and friend was always with me. I was not alone. All had been well with my loved ones. God was so good. So it was back to the busy routine. I didn't think mum noticed I had been absent. Her movements were slow; she took a long time over a meal. She received T.L.C. - tender loving care - from the nursing staff. They started to liquidise her food to make it easier. I really felt it would be better for her to be with the Lord.

Ordination

The I.G.O. Conference in October was very special to me. It had been suggested that I should apply for ministerial status, and I was accepted and was ordained. It was a very moving experience, words of encouragement were spoken over me. I was thrilled as Anna and several of my friends, including one of the elders from Hesketh Bank had come to support me. Brother David Hathaway was also present, and prayed for the sick. Again Anna received ministry. David thought there was a need to fast, and the Hesketh Bank people pledged to join in on Anna's behalf. Praise God for friends who care!

The year was drawing to a close. It was Christmas, we spent time with mum but she was tired. Then the year 1996 begun. Mum was in bed most of the time. She was drowsy, came to, took my hand. I sat, praying that God would take her home. A couple of days later the sister in charge told me mum's body was beginning to break down. This would happen first, then this and this. I can't remember the medical terms. The doctor had given a prescription for medication when discomfort and pain set in. It was 8th January. On the 9th she seemed restless, I spent most of the day in her room. A Christian music tape had been playing in the background. The staff were happy to set it going when I wasn't there.

Standing firm for Mum

As I sat praying, I felt an anger arise in me. This wasn't the victory of Calvary. Mum believed the word "By His stripes we were healed". She had stood firm on many occasions. She had resisted sickness and believed for healing. I recapped in my mind the miracles and healing which had taken place - my dad's cancer gone - the time mum had a bad prolapse, and because of the seriousness of the condition her doctor had sent her to a private consultant. I remembered how she made arrangements for dad if she was hospitalised, but she kept saying, "I'm doing this because my sister's on my back, but Lord, you know I'm not expecting to be in hospital." Dad and she went to the consultant, and after examination he said, "What the xxxx is your doctor about - you've wasted my time. There is nothing wrong." Mum wasn't surprised. It's what she believed for, and besides she had been wakened in the early hours by a "jerk" within her body and knew all was well.

So all these things went through my mind. I felt angry with the devil - he came to steal, to rob and to destroy. The Lord Jesus paid the price of our redemption at Calvary.

The Bible tells us,' He arose from the dead having disarmed principalities and powers' Col. 2:15. The book of Revelation states 'I am He (Jesus) who was dead, behold I am alive for ever more, and I have the keys of Hell and death' Chapter 1:18 . The Bible also tells us that it is appointed unto man to die once, Heb. 9:27, that the last enemy that will be destroyed is death 1 Cor. 15:26. To the Christian, death should just be a passing from life into the presence of God. So I prayed, "Lord, honour my mum in death as You honoured her faith in life. Lord I want to see the victory of Calvary." The restlessness left, mum was still, the sister came in and said she was in a peaceful sleep. She said I should go home and get rest, and promised to phone if things changed. So I obeyed - had a meal.

A presence in the room

About ten I phoned the home, the night sister answered, having enquired about mum she said, "Oh, there is a presence in her room." I remember thinking what kind of a presence, and I said, "Mum is a Christian it can only be good." She replied, "It is, it has made me feel all peaceful and Becky's sleeping. We will phone you if necessary." So I went to bed, went to sleep, also at peace. I awakened about 4.30 a.m., decided to get up, put clean bedding on the other beds, tidy up, get some breakfast, and about two hours later the phone rang. "Please come." I phoned Anna, and we went to the home. Mum was on her back, breathing a bit uneven. Sister said, "We promised to call you when she wakened." Anna said, "I don't want gran to suffer", and with no planned words I went to the bed, put my arms around my mum and heard myself say, "Even so, come Lord Jesus". I stepped back. Mum gave a sigh and was gone. The staff were amazed. They expected her condition to deteriorate - to use the drugs. Anna and I were taken to a small lounge to await the doctor, and while there we had several staff, including management, come and enquire what was different about my mum. We were able to witness for the Lord Jesus, explaining the reality of the gospel, the reality of relationship with God through Christ, rather than a religious experience. It was January 9th, two days before my mum's 92nd birthday.

Another challenge

I felt I hadn't let her down. God certainly hadn't. Again what a mighty God we serve. I rejoiced because mum was with the Saviour she adored. I was sad because she was gone. I had the task of telling the family, another funeral to arrange, her affairs to sort out. This wasn't hard, all her worldly goods were gone, there was just enough to pay the expenses. This money had been another challenge to me. My dad had told me just before he died that he had money to cover mum should she need nursing care. He had also left a gift to Billy, Andrew and Anna - the house and all else to me. However, dad had made his calculations on prices in 1980, and had not foreseen the colossal rise in the cost of care. I didn't grudge mum's money going on her care, but I had to struggle with the fact that they had been careful with spending so as to save for a 'rainy day' and so many people spent all from week to week, and now received full payment from the government. I watched all her savings go. I had to sell the house, watch it all go, £340 per week - listened while others boasted how they had outwitted the system, etc. I can honestly say I was never tempted to do wrong, but I had to allow God to work in me, so it didn't destroy my peace - nor cause me to worry about the future. After all, He is the One who will supply my need. The week before mum died I had filled in a form stating she had less than £3,000 in her bank, and was applying for a government grant. According to her will, Billy, Andrew and Anna received £1,000 each. Billy's automatically came to me and with that I paid the expenses. I had no legacy that dad had planned, but I have another Father - the Heavenly Father - who also cares for me, and that month I received money from my late uncle's estate. I knew I was the beneficiary but hadn't know the extent.

Chapter 25

The Teaching Ministry

At the time of mum's death I was very emotional. My diary tells me I was weepy - tired. Andrew was bad-tempered when I visited him. His carer had brought him to the funeral. Did he miss his gran? How much did he understand? I had no way of knowing. He couldn't speak. He couldn't tell me how he felt. Anna had to visit a chiropractor, I took her and she was in so much pain. I felt helpless but always, always, my cry went out to the Lord. I came through. I turned my 'sights' to the future. Penmaenmawr - the teaching ministry. Was it time to move? Was I to move? Then I remembered the Lord spoke to me from the book of Ruth - I have the date pencilled in my Bible, 11.2.95 - "Sit still my daughter until you know how the matter will turn out." That was then, Lord! It's a year later, but the Lord made it clear in my spirit that word still stood So I had to be content, had to be patient! I felt the urge to change my car. The Sierra ran well, but it was large. I didn't need the big boot - no wheelchair for mum.

One morning I awakened with these thoughts, so I prayed that God would direct my path. I phoned John, the mechanic, he suggested that I try a car dealer at Birkdale.

I went - nothing. I did some shopping then went home. I was determined to spend the afternoon in prayer, and was annoyed with myself because all I could think of was "car". I kept pulling my thoughts back to seeking the Lord. Then the word "Oldfields" came into my mind, with "car", I tried to dismiss this, but it wouldn't go. I decided to go out - walk to a car place near the town centre - I didn't know the name. I felt so excited as I drew near - it was Oldfields. I walked in - saw cars - and one seemed to stand out. An inner voice said, "That's your car". The salesman came, I got the particulars, asked if he would phone John to come and vet it.

Obeying the promptings

I returned home, almost dancing. If not outwardly, certainly within. I called with Craig & Anna to tell them - "Good", they said, "But you don't just take the first car" (I do if God's in it!), "you shop around - you compare mileage and prices" (I don't when God says this one's for me!). "Why don't we visit the Vauxhall dealer round the corner?" I kept my thoughts to myself and to please them, we went. There wasn't a better one John looked the car over and said I had better snap it up. I had a three-year-old car which was as good as new. I had a test drive, paid the deposit, had a "block" not to part exchange. Sorted out insurance, etc., and next day had my car. I wondered if it was to ask John to sell the Sierra, but no - God prompted me to give it as a 'thank offering as unto Him' to a brother who needed a car. So I obeyed.

So the next weeks passed and it was Conference time again. It was good. While in one of the meetings it seemed to register with me that the three areas I had been accused of being false, were the areas that God was using me, namely - being led by the Holy Spirit, prayer and prophecy. I was flooded with a sense of gratitude and praise, and a realisation that's how Satan works. He tries to stop you before you even begin. I think these thoughts came after a fellow minister prayed with me and declared I was causing havoc in the devil's kingdom with the prayer ministry.

Meeting Hazel

It was at this Conference I met Hazel Old. She was alone, and I just offered my company. This was the beginning of a rich friendship. She visited me, and I stayed at her home. Her pastor, the late Ron McCatty would invite me to speak at his church. In the course of time this was the link to North Wales, and Hazel is now working at I.G.O. Headquarters, as are my other friends Stella & Bill. There are so many "what ifs" in life. What if - I hadn't spoken to Hazel? What if - I hadn't offered Stella a lift to Hesketh Bank? God uses people to bring about His purposes. Even as I pen these words, my heart is talking to the Lord. Don't let me miss Your appointments. Don't let me ignore Your prompting.

It was also at this time I received further words of prophecy - I would go to lands where there were sad, unhappy people, and would have angelic protection. The second was - God was bringing me into a place of authority and people would respond. I made notes of these words. Could it be true? "There is nothing in me - it has to be You, Lord. I'm a sparrow, but you can cause me to soar like an eagle." I kept these things in my heart. It was also at this Conference that I led one of the early morning prayer meetings for the first time, at the invitation of Syd Thayre, now with the Lord. He was the prayer co-ordinator at that time.

So, back to routine. Visit Andrew - Anna - take her to clinics, do her housework, shopping - travel to Pen, stop over an extra night. Another thought came to mind - I could do with a room to be on my own - it wasn't fair on Bob & Ann to have to put me up all the time. I can't remember if I voiced this to them, probably I did, then Bob told me a lady had a caravan at the back of her house. He and Ann took me to meet her, and she agreed to let me have it as a very low rental. I could have the key, come and go as I pleased, was allowed friends to stay if I chose. Things seemed to happen so quickly. In April I spent my first night in the van. I found life exciting - what would happen next?

The Joshua Course

May saw the first Joshua Course. I enjoyed teaching. Then the meeting in the Old People's home - the shop - the prayer meetings - and home. Each time I came home, I found Anna had been poorly. I felt guilty that I wasn't there for her. Craig booked a holiday, hoping that some sunshine would do her good. I drove them to the airport on Sunday and got back in time for church. On the Tuesday, I was in town doing some shopping for my elderly neighbour, and as I walked out of the supermarket I heard a voice in my head, "Go now!" It was very clear, and I knew that I knew it referred to me moving to live in Penmaenmawr. So I went into the nearest Estate Agents and enquired about putting my house on the market. I asked that the "For Sale" board wouldn't go up until my daughter was back from holiday.

Bob Searle contacted me by phone and asked if I could come down a bit earlier. A brother in the Lord felt prompted to buy a derelict hotel, and they were meeting in the hotel for prayer before seeing the agent. I left early Wednesday and knew I needed to seek the Lord. I prayed as I travelled, arrived at the caravan just after nine, and felt drawn to read Isaiah 54 - it didn't speak to me. I had no leading - no views whatsoever. I met Bob, Kingsley, and several others at the Puffin Hotel. It was a mess, every window broken, it had been professionally vandalised in my opinion. Lead stripped from roof, water had poured down interior walls - you looked at the ceiling and could see the sky. Floor boards up, wires ripped out, wash basin off the walls, taps missing. We stood in a large room, glass and puddles competing for floor space, and I thought, "No one in their right mind would want to buy this place."

Speaking the word

Bob called us to prayer. Was Dr. Martin's prompting from God? What was God's will? The presence of God was tangible - it was all around us - and suddenly I felt the anointing - the chapter I had read sprang to life - and I knew I was to speak a "prophetic" word. I felt fear - I felt the responsibility - but I had to obey. I remember as if it was yesterday - I don't need my diary account. I said, "Brothers, if you have ever judged a word please judge what I'm about to say", and I began to speak what I felt the Holy Spirit was giving me. The hotel was symbolic, as we saw the place desolate and broken down, that was how God viewed His Church. As we would see the building being restored and beautified - it would be an object lesson of how God would be restoring His Church. As I finished speaking there was silence, then Kingsley spoke. "This is God - we must go for it." All were in agreement. I stood in awe! I am called to be part of the purposes of God in this place.

I went on to my teaching session, and had the privilege of praying with a young man who received the baptism in the Holy Spirit, speaking in a new tongue.

"Go for it!"

Craig and Anna came home. I picked them up at the airport, having driven there from Penmaenmawr. I waited until the next day to tell them I was going to sell the house and move. I think they were shocked. Craig just said, "Go for it." Anna said later that although it came as a surprise, it lurked at the back of her mind that it would happen. She loved the Lord enough to recognise His leading and to free me to go.

So the next weeks were busy. Routine in Southport - visit Andrew - tell the staff - they were also supportive, promising to bring Andrew to visit me. Routine in North Wales - looking for a home - Bob & Ann looking in the papers, etc., - getting keys to view. I wanted a three bedroomed bungalow, wanted to live near "The Oasis", as the Puffin Hotel was to be called. There didn't seem to be anything suitable. I was beginning to think I would have to settle for two bedrooms. One day Ann took me to Cae Gwynan to see one, and I felt closed in and didn't get out of the car to look at it. With hindsight, I believe God was in that decision. The next week there was a three bedroomed bungalow in the paper. On enquiry Ann said she didn't get the key because it was in the place I didn't want. I said I had better look, and discovered it was next door to the one I hadn't viewed, and had an extension built.

As soon as I walked over the threshold I knew it was the one for me. I am sure the Lord kept me from its neighbour, because He knew this one was coming up. Hallelujah. I don't feel I should go into all the details, other than to say that at a time when some houses in Southport had been on the market for twelve months, my "For Sale" sign went up on the 8th June, and I moved into my new home on the 9th September.

Feelings of guilt

I can't begin to describe how guilty I felt about leaving Anna. She never complained, never indicated in any way that I shouldn't move. In fact she was a source of encouragement, advising me on carpets, wallpaper, etc. Craig & Anna had come to see it and Craig said he would do some work for me - install a new kitchen and bathroom. It didn't make me feel better - it was as if something whispered all the time - how mean I was - I cried tears, but I knew I was to go. I was able to get a lady to do some of Anna's housework and heavy shopping. Praise God I was in the position to pay. I felt Anna should come to Conference with me at the end of September. Craig would work in my house. We set off for Swanwick, Anna was in pain all the journey. I felt uptight. I tried to drive smoothly and was aware of every jerk. I was calling out to God. I was confessing the promises - but still pain and more pain.

We arrived and went to the room we were sharing. Anna wanted to be alone so I walked the grounds. I felt the enemy leering at me ... "You say you believe - you're the prayer leader - how can you lead others when you cant get answers yourself?" I wondered how I could take the morning prayer meeting. "But God!" - something arose in me - I WILL

NOT be intimidated by the enemy - it's not me, it's Christ in me - I can be more than a conqueror. I met Brother David Greenow, he asked how I was, so I told him about the battle. He prayed with me, for me and for Anna. I returned to our room. Anna was washing her face - her eyes red from weeping and she said, "Mum - I'm not allowing Satan to win - I'm going to the meeting."

Slain by the power of God

The speaker was David Carr, he came on to the platform declaring there was a healing anointing in the place. He would pray for the sick before he preached. He asked people to come forward for prayer - then he pointed directly to Anna and said, "I want that young woman to come now." Anna went as bid, he had a word of knowledge, was able to describe her pain - the panic attacks - the fear when her chest tightened up. He said, "The panic has gone." Anna was slain by the power of God - she lay on the floor for the rest of the meeting. God the Healer doing something in her body. What if? What if we had succumbed to the enemy's suggestions. What if she hadn't gone to that meeting? What if we hadn't grasped the hand of God to bring us through? What if? Anna didn't receive a complete healing, she still has pain from her neck, but not the panic attacks. The meeting was another turning point and we expect that God will do what His word declares. What He has begun, He will complete.

The next few months flew by. I arranged my home just as I wanted it. I felt so content. I visited Anna, she was so much better. We could enjoy our time together, rejoicing in the goodness of God. It was Christmas once more. I spent it with Craig & Anna, visited Andrew, and returned home on Boxing Day. Craig & Anna came to stay a couple of days with me. What a happy time. God was so good. Another prayer was answered. When I moved I had two cats from them being six weeks old. I wanted to keep them, but wondered what to do when I was away from home. One of my new neighbours heard I had put them in a cat's home while the work was going on and she said I mustn't do that, she would feed them for me. So they had a "home" in the garage and were only in the house when I was. I fed them in the garage and when I was away, Sue or her son Mark fed them. This continued for the next five years. How good is my Heavenly Father, and how good were my neighbours.

A haven of rest

I was at peace, content, it was as if the raging seas had calmed, the storms abated. I was guided to the desired haven, as the Psalmist says in chapter 107:30. Life took on a new routine - help in the shop. Bob asked me to be responsible for the prayer meetings, and sometimes to lead or to speak at the Sunday service. I travelled to Southport quite regularly to see Anna, gave her a helping hand when needed - visited Andrew, and other friends. I praise God I've always made friends, and the real friendship endures. Sometimes I stayed overnight with either Stella, Maureen or Winnie. The latter lost her husband some months after I was widowed and our loneliness drew us together. Friends came to visit me, stayed in my home. I was so blessed.

Chapter 26

Part of the Team

I asked God to fulfil the call on my life, to open doors for ministry. In the February I went to Northern Ireland, taking my car on the Holyhead-Dun Laoghaire Ferry. I was to visit family and friends, but also to speak at several churches. This was exciting. I was leaning on the Lord all the time. When I travelled I was always looking to witness to someone, and this was no exception. A lady and gentleman came to sit beside me. Her intention was similar to mine, only she was a Jehovah's Witness. We had an interesting time and I didn't realise how time had passed until the voice over the tannoy said we were not entering Dublin Bay as there was a freak storm, it would be hours before it lifted. We were given a free meal, and I began to be concerned about time as I had to drive right up to the North. I remember praying, asking the Lord to rebuke the wind and the waves. I had written in my diary, "I felt the Lord say, 'You do it!'" It was 3 p.m. and we weren't expected to dock until 6 p.m. I obeyed this prompting and spoke the rebuke aloud. At 3.15 p.m. the tannoy spluttered to life again and the captain said, "The winds have dropped, we are able to dock." I drove off the boat at 3.45 p.m. I was able to phone my cousin and tell her I would be late. How elated I was. I'm in touch with the Miracle-Working God. He is my Lord.

God's guidance

The adventure wasn't over though. It meant I was driving in darkness instead of daylight. I felt nervous, especially when a lone man stood in the middle of the road and directed traffic off to the right. No explanation. He was dressed in waterproof clothing, in the glance I had there was nothing to indicate what he was. Being in Ireland, thoughts of hijacked cars, etc., raced into your mind. There was a larger truck in front of me. The road was narrow and winding, and unlit. Oh Lord, guide me. Don't let me go wrong. Protect me. I felt I was to follow the truck. This was good, when I saw his rear lights go nearer the hedge I knew there was oncoming traffic. When he turned I followed. Several miles further we approached a junction. I could go three ways, but I obeyed the prompting, and the truck lead back on to the main road. My diary entry states, "Arrived at Lorna's 9 p.m., tired but victorious - God is good."

In June I went to Bristol to visit Hazel and on to minister in South Wales, then back to the routine at home - prayer - the teaching sessions. It all dovetailed together. The restoration of the building had been going steadily. When you realised how much work - the cost - I was always thankful it hadn't been our desire, but rather it was given to N.W.G.O. (North Wales Gospel Outreach), therefore, I was able to throw the need of money, etc., on to the Lord without worry. Bob would say we never had much in the bank but the bills got paid on time. What a faithful God we serve, and I felt so privileged to be part of the team. I never felt at ease when I had to Pastor the fellowship after Billy died. I knew God had told me to and I obeyed, but I always felt God had an order - Christ the head of man, man the head of woman. I had no problem with anyone else, it was just how I felt. So now with no Billy to watch over me, I felt secure in Bob, Kingsley and John's care. They would correct me if necessary. When I went out to minister I went with their blessing, with prayer backing. I made all my decisions before God, and was free to be what God wanted me to be.

Fellowship and fun

In July we began to see people stay at the Oasis, and I helped Ann with the catering. As teaching sessions with the Nehemiah Bible School started, it coincided with a Joshua Course. The leaders decided to take the students to Northern Ireland for the I.G.O. Convention Day. I went too, using my car. Kingsley had his. What fun we had. Bob is always full of humour. We stayed at a fellow minister's church, he had a mobile home so we crowd in - ladies sharing the bedrooms, the men 'camp' in the lounge.

It was during this year that Bob introduced me to Pete Levers and Heart Cry for Wales. A bi-monthly prayer meeting held in Colwyn Bay. I have attended these meetings whenever I am free ever since, and this introduction was another 'happening' in my life.

October brought Conference time in Swanwick once again. Anna came and I felt so proud of her as she lead the worship at the trustees request. Once more another year went by. I spent Christmas in Southport with family. Hazel came to spend the New Year with me. Hallelujah - God be praised. He had kept me and in measure had used me. I was grateful. I looked forward to the next months, a continuation of all that had begun. It took the same format - while at the Oasis, I was invited to minister at Radcliffe, where we once pastored, at Bristol, South Wales, Elim Southport, and back to Northern Ireland. I felt in need of a real break so Hazel and I had an enjoyable coach tour in Southern Ireland - Something I had always wanted to do, as it is such a beautiful country.

There was great excitement in September when Bill & Stella moved to Penmaenmawr, and became members of the team. I personally was thrilled, as I had some input into their lives, as they had in mine. I felt things were 'ticking over' nicely - then I was greatly challenged in my own life.

Ghana

Kingsley and John had taken a team out to Accra, captial of Ghana, to meet and welcome into the I.G.O. Fellowship a young man, Osmond Osei Owusu. They came back, testifying about the experience, how good it was to encourage God's people in Accra, to see people saved. How they worshipped God heartily in their poverty. How hot and humid it was. "You should come next time." "I should go", echoed in my heart. No way! I couldn't stand the heat - nor the spicy food. No! No! Then God brought conviction to me. I felt He spoke in the depth of my being. "Doreen you pray for others that I will help them, I will protect them from harm and sickness. You claim My word on their behalf. Now put your faith where your mouth is - claim the promises for yourself." I had to surrender. I had to repent. I was truly sorry. I couldn't wait for the service to end, and when it did, I told John and Kingsley I would go next time. It was settled. I would go. I was excited. Another step into the promise over my life.

Forty years on ...

For many years I had carried a desire to return to Full Gospel Bible Institute in Canada. Over the years I had received notification of class reunions etc., but never had opportunity nor finance to go. I longed to meet the people who had such spiritual input in my life. Forty years had passed. I wasn't consciously thinking about it, but one day I had a phone call from Art Sheppherd in Vancouver. He felt 'led of the Spirit' to contact me, and say Greta and he were going to Eston early November and if I could get to Vancouver, they would be happy to take me to Eston. My heart leapt within - this was God. I said I would ring him back. I felt I should go. I spoke to Bob, just to confirm I could leave my commitments. Booked a flight from Manchester - Heathrow - Vancouver.

It was good to see Art & Greta, I was able to rent an apartment in the condominium where they had their home. Vancouver was beautiful. Art had booked a flight for us over the Rockies into Banff Alberta. He had hired a car to drive across the state and into Saskatchewan. Oh the wonder of seeing the scenery - the flatness of the bald prairies once again. Eston hadn't changed much, more modern grain silos, paved streets, trees in gardens, but I recognised a lot. Sadly our first little home had gone, but the memories remained.

Art didn't know what else was scheduled other than his time with students. It just 'happened' to be the weekend of reunion. It just 'happened' that the Monday and Tuesday were meetings for pastors from the area. I got to meet many of my year who remembered Billy and me. I was asked to share at the reunion. What joy! What a God to arrange all this for me. To grant me the desire of my heart. Also present was one of the visiting tutors - Pastor Lorme Pritchard. He had taught me so much. We were so pleased to see each other. I was able to spend time at the home of the College President, G.S. McLean and his wife. Both these men were in their eighties, Bro. McLean has since gone to Glory. What a joy it was to be able to thank them personally for their teaching of truth. It was the foundation for the rest of my life. They were also overjoyed to see, as it were, fruit of their ministry. I had gone on to serve the Lord and was still doing so.

Indian Summer

I had taken winter clothing as Eston had a fall of snow, but while there I didn't need my boots or fur hat or gloves. It was a beautiful Indian Summer. As we drove back to Banff the skies darkened and snow began to fall. Art said we had left at the right time. I didn't see the Rockies from the East side. It was completely hidden in the blizzard. We were able to take off as planned, back to Art & Greta's for a few more days. Greta took me sightseeing - what an experience. Soon it was time to fly home. I enjoyed everything, but how glad I was to see Teresa and Stella from the Oasis waiting for me at Manchester Airport.

The latter half of this year brought some changes. Kingsley and family moved back to the North of England. He had received many invitations to do the Joshua Course at individual churches, thus impacting many more people. It meant that I no longer had an input. Then John felt he should change tack, rather than a residential course, have a correspondence school. So again I wouldn't be teaching, although I was asked to rewrite my notes to they could be used. This I was happy to do. I didn't feel perturbed, could see the good sense and wished them well. I had my eyes on the future. Ghana here I come!

Chapter 27

Ghana

I prepared studies for the Ghana trip. John indicated I would be part of the teaching team. I had all sorts of emotions - excitement - apprehension. I got friends to stand with me in prayer, for no sickness, no heat rash, strength to cope. I wasn't close to any ladies who had been, so I relied on the Lord to prompt me what I needed to take. What clothes to wear to help me survive. And He did.

During the week prior to departure one of my cats went missing. It was unusual, they both stay close to home. For days Tinker was not about. I loved my cats and was perturbed. It was also distracting me, and I asked the folk at Oasis to pray that God would undertake. I remember sitting quietly meditating on the Sunday afternoon, and into my mind came the thought, "Go next door and enquire about Tinker." So I got up and went outside. I missed my immediate neighbour and started up the path of the next bungalow - and had a distinct thought "I said next door". So I retraced my steps and knocked at that door. My neighbour came, she hadn't seen Tinker - her garage hadn't been opened for a couple of days, and while we were talking there was 'mewing'. Tinker must have heard my voice.

He had been locked in the garage. He was none the worse for his adventure apart from hungry. How grateful I was, yet again to a Heavenly Father interested in every part of my life - enough to help me locate the cat.

The voyage begins

Then it was time to set off for Ghana. John and I met up with Kingsley and the others. Again I enjoyed the new experiences, but I was not prepared for the heat at 7.30 p.m. when I stepped out of the plane. My skin was immediately damp, my hair clung to my head, and that was how it was night and day until I boarded the plane home. Nor was I prepared for the culture shock. Yes, I had seen shanty type buildings on TV, but this was reality. This was how hundreds of people lived. I tried to take it all in, the crowds, the smells, open sewage, cooking, oil lamps (really tapers in oil burning). Being introduced to Brother Osmond and his team. Shown to our room. I was to share with two other ladies. We had a flushing toilet, water basin and a pipe protruding out of the wall - our shower. No hot water, and not always water flowing.

I received another shock next day. Another Brother and I were taken to our venue. We were to speak to a group of Bible Students. The building had a cement floor, posts holding up a roof, no walls, windows or doors. The heat was almost unbearable. We were a little late in arriving, but these people were praying and praising God. I didn't understand their words, but I understood the intensity. My spirit registers these people know how to pray. Then the thought hit me ... How can I teach them about prayer? I felt what we in the West know in theory, these people experience - corporate prayer. Then I realised so few had

Bibles and were hungry for the word of God. Please God anoint me to feed their hunger.

I was also taught another lesson. John had been saying how wonderful it was to dance. I never saw him dance when at home, but he couldn't wait to get back to join in. I was thinking ... I'll dance at home, but I'm not just dancing because I'm in Ghana and everybody else does! I spoke in the first session, then a break. The people sang, thanking God for His word, and the dancing began. I stood respectably to the side of the pulpit, just watching - when suddenly the anointing hit my feet and I was off. I couldn't get my feet to stop. Brother Arthur Mann, who was with me, said afterwards, I had danced with the same footwork as the Ghanaians. I felt a joy in me. I felt God was laughing. "I'll show you", He seemed to say. I survived the whole days, I ate food I wouldn't eat, thought I didn't like, but I enjoyed it all.

Laughter and joy

I got to know a young man, Pastor Dan. He was my carer and interpreter. A young man of integrity. It was great working as a team, encouraging each other. Again much laughter, and joy seeing people won for the Lord. Soon it was home time, back to the routine, able to share experiences. Even more exciting - God is fulfilling His promise - His call on me. I would go to the nations. Age doesn't matter. He hasn't finished with me yet.

The hymn writer wrote "I stand amazed in the presence of Jesus the Nazarene and wonder how He could love me a sinner condemned unclean." I echo that, but I am also amazed that the Lord God Almighty will speak to me - will impart things directly to me. Often when I am seeking

His face as to what I should speak when ministering, I often dream. I see and hear myself preaching. When I awake I know I have received "the message" to impart. It can be the same when I have to lead a prayer meeting. I seek the Lord with the same intensity, and at times "see" the meeting and know what scripture to use and how to give direction. Sadly, sometimes the outcome I expect doesn't fully happen. I still have a lot to learn to be able to communicate clearly where ever I am, and sometimes some people don't know how to respond.

A warning dream

Sometimes I will awaken with a scripture in my mind, and I will get up and jot it down. Sometimes I will go for a book to get further insight and then back to sleep again. One dream I remember vividly happened some time ago. I saw quite clearly members of The Oasis walking with me along a high narrow path with a dangerous drop to lower ground. I felt the danger, and then I saw a lamb just to the side of me. I reached out my hand and touched it. I felt the texture of its coat under my fingers. Then I awoke. I felt pleased because in the natural I always want to touch animals and they always scamper off.

I got up, dressed, and settled down to my prayer time before the morning service. As I did the Spirit of weeping came upon me and I was unable to quench it. I sobbed and again sensed danger. I knew it related to the Oasis and remembered the dream. I realised I had a choice - phone Bob and say I can't go because of the sobbing, or go and explain in person. I chose the latter. It needed to be prayed through. When it was time to start the meeting, Bob immediately called me to share how I felt. The sobs had stopped, outwardly at least. We all began to pray and ask God for protection. After a while the need to intercede lifted and I knew within my spirit we had touched THE LAMB. Stella confirmed this afterwards. Bob then carried on with the regular meeting. Thank God for a man who can "rightly discern" and give correct direction. We never knew what the danger was, but I believe what ever it was, was diverted because of being forewarned.

The joy of preaching

Time passed with the daily routine. I had invites to speak again at Bristol, also Beaumaris. Back to Bristol, to share experience of Ghana at Andy Paget's church. Back to Northern Ireland and later to South Wales. I enjoy these times. I sometimes say to the Lord, "Am I supposed to enjoy preaching so much?" I am careful to give Him all the praise, to lay at His feet all the tributes and thanks I receive. If it wasn't for the anointing and enabling from the Holy Spirit, I know deep deep within I would fall on my face and be shamed.

Hazel moved from Bristol to join the team. Towards the end of this year, I began to think about teaching. The thought arose, "Even if others have a change of plan, it should not affect what God has called me to do. Just because one door closes, it doesn't mean that other doors don't open." So I began to pray about this. Open the door. I talk it over with Bob and he says, "That's right."

Another event takes place. Bob receives an e-mail from a Brother in the USA who wishes to come to North Wales. He tells me and we pray for God's will. We don't want to miss God. So it seems right that he should come. Bob felt it would be good to ask Princes Drive Baptist Church if they would also invite him to their service. This also was proven to be the correct leading. So Norman Benz, his wife Judy and son Erik, arrived and stayed in my home. They ministered at The Oasis and Princes Drive. They were so easy to get on with, and we fellowshipped and shared together. As he was leaving he told me he could see an Apostolic anointing on me for prayer. I don't think I knew what he meant, but again I made a note of it, and pondered it in my heart. The consequence of his visit was the beginning of a relationship, he and his other son Jonathan returned to take part in a week of prayer the next May organised by the brother in Princess Drive. These prayer weeks have continued each year since.

Back to Ghana

Time went by quickly - the year 2000. I returned to Ghana with another team under Kingsley and John's leadership. Such a welcome. The love, the bond between us, was wonderful. The heat was as hot - perhaps hotter, as we went a week later than the previous year. The blessing was mutual, we taught, shared the word, but we also learned so much.

When I got home one of the Oasis members asked if she could have my notes on prayer as she wanted to learn more. I went to Stella to have them printed out and she said, "Don't just give them, teach them." In spite of my prayer for a door to open, I hadn't thought of that, but then I am slow to promote myself. I spoke to Bob. "Go for it!", was his reply, "To have teaching - a School of the Word - is part of the vision for Oasis". I knew that, but I thought it was for teachers that I looked up to, not me. The outcome - I started in the February and it has continued to the present day and is ongoing. When I am away, John, Bob or David Hughes do the teaching. Others have come to enjoy the word of God. I'm blessed. I fall at His feet amazed at His grace.

House of Prayer

I mentioned earlier Heart Cry for Wales. I got to know Pete and flow in the prayer. He felt there was to be a conference for women and I was asked to be part of the organising committee. My emphasis would be prayer. It was great to work with people from other churches. Once again, I believed God gave me the strategy. It was to be "as well as" and not "instead of". With this in mind I approached the leadership from Aglow, Lydia and churches from Anglesey to Holywell. Bob said we could meet in The Oasis, again it was fulfilling part of the vision to be a House of Prayer. We met, leading up to the conference, on a monthly basis and covered the actual conference with continual prayer. When it was over, I felt that there was more to this than just conference. I asked the others and most felt the same, so we re grouped, calling ourselves the Covenant Prayer Group, and this too is still continuing. There was another conference the next year, and prayer was already in place.

At one of our seminars at The Oasis a visiting pastor was present at a prayer time, and that opened the door for me to speak at his fellowship in the Crewe area for a series of meetings. I returned to minister in South Wales and other invitations came from churches in North Wales. I pray that this account doesn't appear to be boastful, but my heart is to encourage any reader who has a desire to serve the Lord, who perhaps has received 'a word' from the Lord, but it doesn't seem to have come about. Don't give up - water the word with prayer, look for it to come to pass. God is no respecter of persons. If He can do it for me, He can do it for you.

Chapter 28

To The Nations

In November we went to Majorca. Bob and Ann had organised a holiday convention. Relaxation during the day, encourage the church in the evening. It was a blessed time, meeting new people, fellowshipping, sharing the word, having fun. Home, another year drew to a close. I was a happy, fulfilled person. The Lord Jesus was the centre of my life.

Christmas time once again. Andrew was brought down by a care worker to spend a day with me. Craig & Anna were going abroad for some sun. I was to spend Christmas Day on my own. Most Oasis folk were away with friends and family. Friends in Southport invited me, but I stayed at home. I invited a lady I knew in Dwygyfylchi to share dinner with me. I didn't mind my own company. I'd lived with me for a long time! A New Year dawned. What would it hold? I didn't know, but I did know Who held my future.

I went back to Ghana, again with Kingsley and John. Other team members were new. It was good to meet all our friends there once again. Wonderful opportunities to minister. This time we also visited Kumasi, north of Accra, met new people and had new experiences. It was hot and this time there was a water shortage. We had a bucket for our daily needs - wash, flush toilet, etc. It made life more difficult but God gave grace. Towards the end of the visit some of the team fell sick, and others had to take their place at different venues. The day before our departure we were invited to the Parliament House to meet the speaker. One route, I felt the heat and felt sick, and was sick when I returned to our digs. Sadly I wasn't able to keep my speaking engagement. I was poorly all the next day, and was glad to board the plane in the evening.

Disturbing the enemy

All the team members had been ill, some still were, apart from one. This hadn't happened before. At Kumasi when Kingsley was preaching, I felt he had spoken a prophetic word and I also felt he had disturbed the enemy. I remember sharing this at our supper table and one brother prayed. In the light of the team sickness I have wondered if I hadn't prayed the warning through. I blamed myself for not being diligent in prayer. I had been claiming the promise Mark 16, "If we drink any deadly thing it shall not hurt you". I felt that included food. There was divided opinion when I got home, many intercessors agreed with me and promised a better prayer shield for next time. One thing, I was determined this experience would not hinder me going again. I had taken these precious people on my heart and had a strong desire to encourage and support them.

Life went on. I enjoyed being busy. I was so glad that I was a Christian. I just couldn't imagine life without the Lord. The weeks continued in much the same routine, until May when I got another surprise! I was at the Heart Cry meeting, and towards the end we went into small groups to pray together. One lady whom I did not know came to me, and she said she saw me looking into a pool, clear like a mirror, and whatever the Lord would say to me, I was to affirm. I weighed these things up, and believed God was in it, and I began to think about it. I decided the only 'pool' I would be able to look at would be the mirror of God's word, and I was convinced the Lord had some correction for me. This was the 'Prayer for Wales' week so the next evening found me in the Baptist Church, again in prayer. I found myself flat on my face before God and used the opportunity to ask God to search me, and reveal anything which needed to be put right, and I was totally surprised to hear the voice in my inner man, which I know, say, "You will receive an invitation to visit Florida."

Florida

I remember saying, "Lord, if this is what I've to affirm - I affirm it." I went home wondering what this meant. What was God up to? The next evening I was at the Oasis but Friday saw me back to the Baptist Church. I wanted to hear Jonathan Benz speak. I was surprised to see his father Norman come across the church to greet me. He hadn't been expected, but had come to support his son. Then Norman said to me, "Judy and I would love to have you visit us. Can you come? Pray about it." I said I would pray, but I was dancing inside. I knew the answer. I would go. I had affirmed it before God!! I shared this with Bob & Ann and they encouraged me. I gave Norman the answer - yes - and he said to come when it suited me. I began to ask my Father to help and guide me regarding time, travel, etc. I found myself thinking I was near enough to visit Alabama - Terry & Janice! So I phoned them. "Yes, come!" The word 'Greyhound' was in my thoughts. I remembered there was a bus service of that name from over forty years ago. Was it still running? "Yes", was the answer. Terry said he would see if there was a flight to be easier, but I knew it was travel with Greyhound.

I found a helpful girl in a travel agency, and I got a flight booked for November from Manchester - Philadelphia - Miami. It was the earliest I could go. I had other commitments, and I didn't want to go August when it would be hot. It was also a cheaper time to fly, especially as it was not a direct return. I was coming home from Atlanta.

Another witnessing opportunity

The time soon passed. I was relaxed, happy and busy, prayerfully preparing for whatever the Lord had in store for me. Bob and Stella had both spoken a 'word' over me, and I knew I would have 'God appointments' and many would be on a one-to-one basis, and I may not even be aware of the happening. I was to fly out two months after the 'September 11th' atrocity, some folk wondered if I was nervous but I had the assurance I was safe in God's will. Hazel drove me to Manchester Airport, and I boarded the plane with excitement and wonderment. This was really happening to me. I marvelled at the lack of fear, the closeness I felt to my God. I sat beside a young man who was studying some notes. I prayed if it was God's will I would be able to witness to him. After a while he closed his book and struck up a conversation. I got my opportunity to testify, found myself speaking about Andrew. It transpired he was going to a conference in the US and asked if he could quote my experience. He didn't know my name, but he did know of my reliance on the Saviour.

Because of heightened security, I had to claim my luggage at Philadelphia and join a long queue to check into the flight to Miami. I remember standing in the crowded hall, and experiencing such peace. It was as if I was detached from all the hassle and anxiety about the passing of time. After nearly an hour, I was through the proceedings, but had quite a lengthy walk to the gate. A black lady came by driving a little two seater buggy. "Want a lift? I'm going where ever you need to go." My God was watching over me. He had every detail under His control.

Secure in God

I duly arrived at Miami, my friends were there to meet me. It was so different from any other air terminus, it was empty apart from the others from my flight, a few airport officials, and guards with rifles. Judy told me that there was so much fear, people would not travel and were keeping their distance from aircraft. It made me realise all the more how secure I was in God.

Both Norman & Judy made me feel so welcome and comfortable in their home at Palm Beach Gardens. It was good to meet up with Erik and Jonathan again. I had the privilege to share with a group of students, the presence of God was very real in our midst. Judy was often busy with church work, in those times she arranged for some sister in the Lord to take me for breakfast, or lunch, or sightseeing. This meant I met several different women and had time for fellowship, exchanging testimonies.

One of these ladies said she had a strong impression from the Lord that I was to 'write' and God would give me words to tell my story which has been on my heart for a

long time, and I felt this gave me the knowledge it was
time to start.

Divine appointment

Norman & Judy were to host a programme on Trinity
Broadcasting TV. I was invited to go with them! This
was a great experience for me to see the inside of a studio,
and be in the audience of a live broadcast. Afterwards they
were meeting for lunch with a pastor and his wife from
Miami area, again I was made so welcome. I realised they
were discussing business so I just sat quietly enjoying my
meal, when the thought came to me, why am I here? So I
was praying "Lord, there must be some purpose!" It just
seemed seconds later when the pastor's wife turned to speak
to me, and out of that conversation she felt I was to come
and speak to their Intercession Group.

I had planned to leave Florida the next day, but I hadn't
got my ticket as Norman was investigating if there was
another way for me to travel rather than the Greyhound
Bus, so Judy said to stay over, and so it was arranged I
would be at the church. Judy arranged that one of the ladies
would drive me part of the way, meet with another of their
ladies, and she would take me the rest of the journey, be
with me at the meeting and then drive me back to Palm
Beach Gardens. Again I enjoyed the fellowship, the
sharing, the scenery.

It was a wonderful meeting. The worship lifted us into
the Heavenlies. I felt the Holy Spirit's anointing and great
liberty while speaking. I was asked to pray with individual
people and felt God prompt me to invite my escort, Karen,
to join with me. I never experienced anything like it before,
we flowed together, the words of knowledge came. What

was different, it came jointly. Karen would begin and I would finish, then it happened in reverse. These words were meaningful to the hearers and there was great rejoicing. One such word, Karen said to one lady, "I see the Lord giving you fish, you're catching them in your hand," and I felt to add, "They are tiddlers, small fish." Neither of us knew this lady was in charge of children, she ran a Christian Day School. I felt the awesome presence of God, and knew this was one of His appointments.

Back on the Greyhound

The next day it was time for goodbyes. There wasn't any easier way to travel to get me to Montgomery, so it was the Greyhound Bus. I wasn't surprised, I had felt all along I was to go Greyhound and have another 'appointment'. A young woman chose to sit beside me, and I felt in my spirit she wasn't the right person. So I just prayed that God would sort it out. A little later she indicated she would move to another seat and as soon as she did, a lady from the rear of the bus came and asked if she could join me. I had the witness, this was right. It was great, we got on so well. We laughed, talked, she pointed out birds, trees, etc., which I would have missed, explained the history of the area for me. She stood in a queue to order food for me at one of the stops. I was really blessed. Throughout the chat she asked questions - Where did I come from? Why was I in Florida? And I had opportunity after opportunity to witness for the Lord Jesus, share the truth of the gospel and challenge her to accept Jesus.

The hours passed so quickly. We parted at Tallahassee. She was meeting her daughter. I was to change buses to travel on. She gave me a hug and told me she needed to hear what I said. Then she said something which really surprised me, and it was this. "When you smiled at me across the waiting room at Palm Springs I just knew I had to speak with you." I hadn't remembered I had smiled. Oh Lord, what a little thing - a smile - but what an outcome. It was days before I realised we hadn't exchanged names or addresses.

The children of promise

The rest of the journey was uneventful, but I was satisfied. I spent it talking to my Lord, dozing and then it was Montgomery, and Terry was waiting for me. I had been on buses for 15 hours. It was wonderful to be with Terry & Janice once again. To meet Christi Michelle, the child of promise and her little brother Joshua. They weren't content with one - God's promise to them was 'you shall have children'. I was invited to minister at their meetings, and it was a joy to encourage the saints and speak into the situation. My visit coincided with Peter and Ida's winter visit, and we enjoyed the fellowship of good friends together.

Soon it was time to pack my suitcase and journey home. The family left me at Atlanta City. When I checked in, I was praying and praising God for His presence and protection. The clerk asked if I was alone. I told him, yes. He said he would change my seat booking to be nearer the exit as the plane would be delayed, and I could be one of the first off. So I made my way to the departure gate. It was well signposted, but in spite of knowing I was at the correct gate I had the urge to ask if I was correct, and I obeyed this urge. On enquiring the answer was affirmative, but again I was asked if I was travelling on my own. When

I said I was, I was asked if they could make different arrangements for me. I knew God was looking after me and I said yes, but why? Apparently the flight was being delayed so long, the attendant thought I would miss the flight out of Philadelphia, so he got me a seat with a different company, flying direct to Manchester. The only difference it made to me was that I had two extra hours in Atlanta. No problem - a book, a coffee, time to reflect on the goodness of God. Again I just basked in His peace, I felt safe, no fear.

Hazel was to meet me, and I had no way of letting her know. I think she was a little alarmed when I didn't appear, and when she had me paged another Mrs. Moore showed up! My flight arrived about thirty minutes later and all was well. I soon settled back to the routine, Christmas came and went, and it was time to prepare for Ghana.

Chapter 29

Ghana Again!

We left mid-January, with Kingsley and John our team leaders. Renewed our fellowship with our Ghanaian brothers and sisters, four of us were teaching in Bible Schools and seminars, whilst the others had open air crusades. These were well attended and many came forward to accept Christ as their Saviour. One evening Kingsley was led by the Holy Spirit to pray for the sick first, to demonstrate the reality of our God, the One True God. Many responded. I prayed with one young man who had broken his leg, couldn't afford hospital treatment, thus it had set wrongly and he couldn't bend and was in constant pain. This was relayed to me by a pastor's wife who was interpreting. I asked if I could lay my hands on his leg and he was able to use the leg normally without pain. There were many others who were healed. When the meeting was over, quite a while later, as the gospel had been preached, people again responded. One man hobbled to the platform. He had been on the fringe, but heard the call for the sick, he had taken a long time to get to us. Several of the brethren prayed with him, told him to be there next night. He came back healed and gave his life to the Lord.

I always seem to have a trial of faith when I'm there. This time it was a bite on the palm side of my hand, just above the wrist. It was annoying, began to throb and a red line began to travel up my arm. By supper time it had travelled about three inches. Some of the team felt I should go to the hospital, and I could understand why. I was in a foreign land and they felt responsible for me. But I had a deep conviction within that I couldn't go. Kingsley had preached about the God who heals, many of the people, in fact most, had no money for doctors, or even medicine, and I felt I needed to trust this God for me. So it was agreed to respect my stand, but if things weren't improved by morning it was to be reviewed. I went to bed trusting God, was able to sleep and when I awakened, looked at my arm fully expecting it to be better, but it was worse - the red line had thickened and doubled in length. Now it was not just a conviction, I felt a stubbornness. I was trusting God! I said, "Lord, I'm going out of my room and the first person I see I'll ask for a prayer of agreement." So I got dressed and went into the entrance hall just as Emmanuel was coming in. So prayer was agreed, and the redness began to receded, and a few hours later was completely gone.

Morning prayer

On this visit I was able to return to an early morning prayer meeting with another team member and Emmanuel. We left at 4.30 a.m. These people meet to pray before going to work! Some had been saved at a street meeting we had held on a previous visit. On this occasion I was able to meet twins and their mother. The previous year they had been carried by their mum, two years old and had never stood on their own feet. I had been asked to pray. I could only respond by throwing myself on God's word. As I had laid my hands on them the power of God came upon the mother and she began to spin round. I'd had to leave and hadn't heard any news regarding them. Now, twelve months later, here they were running around, normal three-year-olds. I was told they got strength into their legs just days after prayer, and began to walk. What faith these dear people have, they haven't been taught to reason with God's word, just believe!

Seeking a companion

I come away from these visits greatly challenged, and I learn so much. Because the crusades went well, it was decided to repeat and extend next year. It was also decided to split the team. The evangelistic thrust would go in January, and the teaching team would go later, perhaps in July. John indicated he couldn't go this July, so it would be eighteen months before returning. I felt disappointed and people said they were aware of it. The week after we were back, Bob asked why I didn't go back this July, and instead of feeling 'I couldn't', something arose within me and I felt 'Oh, could I!'.

I prayed about this, and asked the Lord if it was His will that Osmond would reply to me in a certain way. Osmond was in the UK to attend an I.G.O. Missionary weekend. I spoke to him on the phone, and his answer was what I needed to hear. I then decided I needed a companion, and asked God to raise up the right person. I felt strongly it wasn't to be my choice but His. Bob had already contacted the travel agency and they had two seats at a reduced fare, and could hold them for three days. I had talked with John, as I felt I wanted his blessing seeing he was the team leader. So I went to speak to him again to let him know I was going, and wanted a companion. He said, 'Why not Sandra?' (his wife). I felt he was joking. Sandra had never intimated in my hearing that she had any desire to go. I didn't take the suggestion seriously, but that night I kept waking up and each time a positive reason why it would be good to have Sandra popped into my thinking, by morning I had several reasons and felt it was God.

Confirmation

I shared this with Bob & Ann and decided to phone Sandra when I returned home. I had an errand to do first, so I set off. Then I heard God speak - "Go to Sandra's house now." So I obeyed, turned in the direction of her home. She was in and I told her my heart as I've described above. Her reaction was so positive. "This is God wanting to include me. If it is Him, He will supply my fare, etc." I asked her to pray and give me an answer as soon as she could. I didn't pressurise by mentioning the plane seats. However, she said "Yes" the next day. Bob confirmed our plane seats, and Ghana ... here we come!

In the meantime I had Northern Ireland on my mind. I had been invited back to the churches I had visited before. So an itinerary was arranged. I was able to speak at twelve different meetings as well as spend some time with my cousin and other friends. I was really blessed, and gifts were received so I could travel to Ghana and support the ministry there. It felt different this time. I didn't have either John or Kingsley to lean on and I realised Sandra would be looking to me for guidance. I prayed much, asking God for wisdom, that I would be sensitive to the Holy Spirit.

We got on well together, and the Ghanaians who knew John were delighted to welcome his wife. The weather was a few degrees cooler, but still too hot for my comfort. I was believing the Lord for protection against mosquito bites, with recollections of the last episode. However, the trial of faith took a different turn. The first night in bed I felt three 'nips', and over the next days some more. Apart from a little itch it didn't bother me too much, then suddenly they erupted with tiny blisters. When one came just below my eye I asked a pharmacist what it was. He said I was allergic to whatever had bitten me. He gave me a tablet and Sandra prayed, and once again I received help. The blisters disappeared, and I had no further bites.

Apart from the Sundays when we both ministered at different churches, Sandra and I visited the Bible Schools and seminars together. She testified, or brought a word of exhortation, then I would follow with a teaching session. I was very aware of her prayer for support.

"No Mama, more!"

New doors opened for me. I was invited to speak at a 'before work' prayer group for bank workers from different church backgrounds. I was also asked to speak at a ladies group, and Sandra shared. We were well received and it was decided to hold a seminar the day before we were due to leave. Osmond said to go ahead. So, because of confusion over timing, we went to the early prayer meeting without breakfast. Arrived at the next venue in good time. There were well over 100 people present. Sandra again gave testimony, and I began to teach about prayer, as I had been requested. At the end of an hour I stopped, but it was ... "No Mama, more!" So I continued for nearly another hour.

Then I was asked to pray for the congregation. I was ready to pray, when again ... "No, no Mama, lay hands on each person!" I must admit my heart sank. I was so hot, had been on my feet for hours, apart from the taxi ride. The people lined up in an orderly fashion. Sandra and I prayed with each person in turn, often the Lord would give me a word for an individual. Towards the end, I felt faint. I knew I had to sit down or I would drop. I told Sandra to carry on and went to my chair, put my head as far down as I could, praying I wouldn't pass out. I didn't. I explained to the prophetess in charge and asked her to apologise to the people.

Get me to the gate on time!

There were a couple of interesting things as we travelled. The first occurred in Amsterdam en route to Accra. We had gone to the appointed departure gate - we had both seen the correct information in English at the gate, and had sat down to await departure. I began to feel uneasy and felt I needed to ask if we were at the right gate. Sandra said it was written up, but I still felt uneasy. I made my way over and asked what seemed a silly question, but the answer came, the departure gate had been changed. Thanks to that prompting we had plenty of time to get to the new one.

Something similar happened on the way home. This time in Accra. We were flying to Amsterdam, changing to a flight to Manchester, and our luggage was going to our final destination. Osmond came to see us safely on our way, and carry the heavy cases. Our cases were weighed and labelled, then again I felt to ask another apparently silly question ... "We don't have to claim our luggage at

Amsterdam, do we?" The girl looked at our tickets, looked at the label, looked at the computer and said, "Oh, there's some mistake!" She had to get one case back, it had gone on the belt, and both cases were re-labelled. What a good, loving, Heavenly Father. I am so glad I can hear His prompting. I sometimes wonder what I miss because I get so occupied with self, but I'm learning to rely on Him more and more.

So, once again it was safely back home. Warm water, soft bed, no biting bugs, but a very happy, contented Doreen, grateful for all the wonderful opportunities I had to serve the King of Kings.

Chapter 30

In Parliaments

I had a few days holiday with my friend Winnie from Hesketh Bank. It was good to relax and enjoy the beauty of the Lake District. Other friends came to stay with me. I attended the I.G.O. Day Conference in Belfast and also the one at Swanwick, ever ready to gossip the goodness of my Saviour.

I was greatly surprised one morning when the post brought me an invitation to attend the Prayer Breakfast at the Houses of Parliament in London. I was able to arrange to travel with Winnie, as she attends the monthly meeting regularly, and knew the venues etc. It was a wonderful experience for me. I hadn't been in the capital since childhood - I enjoyed the visit immensely - especially hearing Billy Graham's daughter Ruth giving the message from God's word. It was also wonderful to hear M.P.'s from all parties affirm their faith in Christ.

The end of November brought me another surprise - a phone call - would I re-consider my decision regarding Ghana. I had decided I wouldn't go on the next mission, even though Pastor Dan was to be married. I felt I needed to respect the team leaders' decision to divide the teams. However, I was told the Ghanaian folk would miss me,

John and Kingsley didn't object, and I felt that for some reason God had opened the door. So I said YES. Years ago I had promised the Lord that if He opened a door I would go through. It was only about six weeks until the departure date, would there be a seat on the plane? I felt in my spirit there would be. Would God supply my fare etc? Yes, I believed He would. Please Lord - I don't want to go empty-handed - there is so much need - let me go able to help someone! - to be an answer to their prayer. I was excited, elated, amazed, inside I felt like the man who was healed - leaping and praising God.

Great joy

There was a seat on the plane from Amsterdam, and i got a flight from Manchester in good time to join the other team members. Money came for all my expenses and I didn't go 'empty-handed'.

Once again I experienced great joy as I stepped off the plane, to be greeted by Ghanaian friends. Our team bonded together very quickly, even though many had not met before. Kingsley asked me to led the prayer times.

We travelled to Kumasi, some five hours by road. The crusades were backed by the Presbyterian Church, dedicated brothers and sisters in the Lord. I appreciated this, as my roots in childhood and salvation in Christ began in a Presbyterian Church in Northern Ireland. It was good to see people respond to the Gospel message and make a decision for Christ, and to see many experience the healing power of God in their bodies.

On the Sunday morning we were presented with gifts and then taken to various branch churches. Gary, one of the team members, and I went to one deep in the country -

Mpatasie, where most of the adults and children had never seen a white face. With the help of an interpreter, Gary spoke to the children and I was able to preach the Word to encourage the church.

Late afternoon we travelled back to Accra, felling tired but elated to be part of God's purpose. Again we settled into our rooms. Some of us had company - large cockroaches, mosquitoes - and two of the team had rats visit their room, another frightening experience! At times the water supply was off, also the electricity, that meant no fan, and it was very uncomfortable with the high humidity.

A Christ-centred banquet

What a privilege to sit and chat with the Speaker of the majority party in government. He said I could call him 'Poppa'. He loved the Lord Jesus and was quick to testify of his faith, as were many of the other M.P.'s present at the banquet hosted by I.G.O. It was truly a Christ-centred occasion used to launch the celebration of ten years of democracy. The next day we were invited to attend the opening session of Parliament and to partake of refreshments afterwards.

I returned to the early morning prayer meeting, rising at 4 am. I received a warm welcome and saw the children who walked because of answered prayer. There was the usual wonderful time of praise and intercession followed by worship. People prostrated themselves on the dusty ground or knelt in God's presence. It was truly awesome! Later I was asked to speak and shared thoughts from the Lord's Prayer - that we would allow our relationship with the Father to deepen.

Again there was a good response to the gospel challenge at the open-air crusades. Osmond, our local I.G.O. man, had brought people together from different churches to form a choir. Their singing was so anointed, the presence of God was so real.

Pastor Dan's marriage

The highlight for me was Pastor Dan's wedding, the young man I met when I first visited Accra. I loved this man, his dedication and integrity. As with all others working in Jamestown, money is scarce, and Dan hadn't the money to provide a house or a dowry for his bride. The Lord used me to bring awareness of this need when I returned home and thanks to the response of caring people, Dan got a home fit for a bride. I was asked to attend the betrothal ceremony. Dan was not present at this meeting at all, but their two families met to agree that the dowry etc. was acceptable. Then Elizabeth, the bride, was brought in and I was given the privilege of placing the ring on her finger, then, to show that she was given to and accepted by Dan's family, she was seated on my knee. I was overcome, first by the great honour bestowed on me, and by the grace of the Almighty God to open the way for me to be in Ghana at this special time. Later, at their Christian marriage ceremony, I was also honoured by being asked to help the couple cut their wedding cake and to share a few words.

I had decided not to go to Ghana for the right reason - respect for leadership. *But God ...!* once again I could trace His hand, leading, guiding, protecting, keeping me in good health. I haven't words to express my gratitude to my Lord.

Chapter 31

Not Finished Yet ...

My story is up to date. I have tried to be honest in the telling, not to exaggerate; to rely on the Holy Spirit as best as I know how, what events to include and what to leave out; and above all, to trust that in this story Jesus will be seen. It is not finished yet. It will not finish, but go on into eternity where I shall at last see Jesus my Lord and Saviour face to face. I don't know what the future holds, but I anticipate more opportunities, more adventures of faith, and the outworking of the continual promise over my life.

I am seeing prophecy over my life being fulfilled, doors are opening for me to travel. I return to Northern Ireland, and have received an invitation to New Brunswick in Canada. The Lord willing, I hope to join John's team to return to Ghana later in the year. I am believing to have the right word for the right people, at the right time in the right place! After all, God has promised to "put His words in my mouth".

Sixty-nine years have passed since my mother 'gave' me back to God. I give God all the glory and all the praise. When I look back I don't think I would wish anything had been different. Oh yes, with hindsight, with the measure of maturity I have now, I would have reacted in better ways. I do know that all the ingredients in my life - the ups and the downs, the joys, the sorrows, times of desperation, the need to throw myself on God's grace - have all contributed to who I am now. When I look deeply into myself, when I look at Christ in the word, I realise I've still a long way to go to be Christ-like. I'm glad He is not finished with me, and will continue to change me.

I don't know who will read this story, but I can't close without a challenge. If you don't know Jesus as your personal Saviour, please realise we have all sinned, all fallen short of God's glory, we can't improve ourselves, sin must be judged and God Himself took that judgement. It was God manifested in the flesh - Jesus Christ - who bore our sin and sickness when He was crucified at Calvary. He arose from the dead, and lives that we may have life - abundant life - eternal life - a home in Heaven, no more sin, sickness, sorrow, death or tears. Trust Him!

I wouldn't trade my life in Christ for anything. I have found Him to be a faithful God. Even through times when I faltered or let Him down, He was always there. And I share the confidence that He always will be. I pray for continual grace to live a life pleasing to Him, and only He knows how long that will be here on this earth - and with that I am content.

Post-script ...

It broke my heart when my dear friend 'Auntie' told me that our friendship was finished. I thought that was the end ... *But God* ...*!* I am so thrilled to be able to say that, just a matter of weeks before the publication of this book, that my wonderful Lord has brought about reconciliation and the renewal of our friendship. What a faithful God we serve!